f. d. maurice

a study

International Standard Book Number: 0-936384-05-0
Library of Congress Catalog Number: 82-70636

Printed in the U. S. A. by Shea Brothers, Inc.
Cover photograph: Jane Redmont

F. D. MAURICE

A STUDY

FRANK McCLAIN

RICHARD NORRIS

JOHN ORENS

cowley publications

chronology

1848   failure of Chartist Movement and formation of Christian Socialists with Ludlow, Kingsley, and others
Politics for the People
founding of Queens College, Harley Street, a college for women

1849   marries Georgina Hare

1850   *Tracts on Christian Socialism*

1853   publication of *Theological Essays*, "eternal life" controversy, and removal from King's College

1854   founding of the Working Men's College, London

1859   attack on Mansel's Bampton Lectures with *What is Revelation?*

1860   appointed to St. Peter's, Vere Street

1866   appointed Knightbridge Professor of Casuistry, Moral Theology and Moral Philosophy at Cambridge

1871   appointed Chaplain, St. Edward's, Cambridge

1872   dies in London

contents

foreword

This study of Frederick Denison Maurice, the nineteenth-century Anglican theologian and reformer, is not intended as a work of historical theology, nor as a vignette of social and religious life in Victorian England, nor even as a portrait of Maurice himself. It is instead a series of sketches for a portrait, three quick studies of the man from different angles; it is an attempt to catch, as we say of sketches, his likeness. It was undertaken in the belief that Maurice's thought is even more compelling in our day than in his own. We are all living in the very landscape, both inner and outer, emotional and physical, that Maurice describes — a landscape that confirms his sense of a "very hopeless kind of darkness," the danger we face when we live alone, apart from neighbors and friends and enemies and apart from the life of God incarnate. It is the darkness Maurice warned us we would encounter if we try to live one hour apart from Christ, and it is a danger humans have always faced. The Industrial Revolution certainly did not cause it, although the stark images of the machine age do highlight human solitude and Maurice's sense of perennial human loss.

It is easy now to recognize some of the things Maurice warned us about over a century ago, but this very ease may prove to be a stumbling-block. Ideas original, even startling then, have become our commonplaces: his ecumenicism, his hatred of divisiveness and strife, his embracing of women's causes, his rejection of rigorism. In our own time we pay lip-service, at least, to the importance of these convictions, where we do not give them our passionate concern. So it is easy to lose sight of Maurice's urgency for us, to lose sight of the fact that he is not "about" any of these issues any more than he is "about" the perils of industrialization or the effects of shifting population patterns on churchgoing. This is merely the outer edge. What Maurice can teach us about is *sociability* in the deepest sense of the word — relationship, connectedness, the ties between human and divine that are created in the sociability of the kingdom of God. Apart from the kingdom of Christ, Maurice tells us, things atomize, split, and fall away; they are pulled from the center as if by centrifugal force. It is this vision he bequeaths to us at a particularly appropriate time in our own history.

In *The Victorian Church* Owen Chadwick tells a story which points up very well the nature of the gulf between that world and ours. During Christmastide of 1853, he relates, nearly a thousand working men gathered at Castle Street in London in order to present Maurice with an address. They had assembled, they said, because "it was extremely creditable to the Reverend Mr. Maurice that he had given a more liberal, merciful, and genial interpretation to the Holy Scriptures than was usually given to them, and on this account the working classes were grateful to him" (1:549). Quite apart from the fact that Maurice's "genial" readings of Holy Scripture had cost him his job at King's College earlier that year, how are we to take this story, so Victorian and so incredible? The gratitude of the working poor for being released from the Church's stand on eternal punishment by Mr. Maurice having redefined "eternal" is certainly edifying, yet it seems to come to us from a great distance.

The Maurice legend is rife with such stories, many of them the stuff of hagiography, and hence they pose difficulties when we try to arrive at some perception of the man himself. The gulf seems to widen even as our imaginations are provoked by the stories, with all their Victorian fixtures — the "little bands" of faithful disciples, the deathbed scenes, the bouts of scrupulousness and self-denial, the Bible classes for day laborers, the difficult sisters, the acts of philanthropy, the querulous second wife who styled herself an invalid and spent fifty years in bed. There are the anecdotes about Maurice's writing of his books, giving dictation while flourishing a red-hot poker, and the hours spent at the bedsides of mother and sisters. Perhaps what separates us most from Maurice is our sense of the qualities that lie behind these stories, and by that I mean his goodness, his charity, the humility and self-effacement that the anecdotes uncover.

All this is only another way of saying that Maurice was very much a person of his times, very much a mid-Victorian, and hence he is "dated" in the best sense of the word. Human consciousness and human perceptions change. The Victorians were not very much like us, point though we will to the appearance of learned agnosticism in the early nineteenth century, beginning with its discovery that Genesis and geology did not agree. When John William Colenso, the bishop of Natal, examined the first five books of the Bible and decided that none of them was written by Moses or anyone else "acquainted personally" with the facts, he was tried for heresy. D. F. Strauss wrote a life of Jesus which found what he called "mythology" in connection with the gospels, and it led to his losing his fellowship and his faith together. When the furor over geology had died down, and geological inquiry became the respectable hobby of High Church clergy, then the furor over evolution started with the publication of Darwin's *The Origin of Species* in 1859.

The situation was more complicated than that, for disaffection with the Church could not be considered widespread at the time and atheism was still a novelty. In Maurice's day religion had a grip on the middle-class imagination, and on popular culture itself, that is important to recognize. Religion in one form or another furnished much of the plot material for writers of popular fiction: there were Tractarian novels, Evangelical novels, Roman Catholic novels, Broad and High and Low Church novels, as well as novels that attacked all of these. The quintessential romance of the period, Mrs. Humphrey Ward's *Robert Elsmere*, is about a clergyman who resigns his pulpit when he can no longer believe; the popular literary villain of the time was the "Jesuit," usually Italian; there was even the "Jesuitess," who engaged in Satanic mischief too appalling for most novelists — usually clergymen and women — to describe at all. To come at it from the opposite angle, the Victorians thought it important to mention that George Eliot was the first great "godless" writer of English fiction; "godlessness" was not a quality they took for granted.

These Victorians were curious, and they were frightened, and they felt themselves to be standing on the edge of an immense void. Buoyed up by a sense of greatness and confidence, by the increasing territorial expansion of the British Empire and by unprecedented industrial growth, the Victorians were thus set free to become curious. They were curious about fossils, about hypnotism, about the height and weight of Noah's ark, about the South Seas and natural monstrosities and chemistry and death. Yet gratification of this curiosity gave way to another, less buoyant mood, and one that had to do with a sense of deprivation, a fear that through no fault of their own they had been exiled and cut off from some significant and life-giving purpose. As their control over the commercial and public spheres of life increased, the Victorians feared a corresponding loss of touch with other, more inward and private satisfactions. The poetry of the period expresses this fear in images of confusion, strife, warfare, exile, and the human soul is pictured as lost, strayed, or abandoned; it is an orphan, or a foundling child. It is at this point that we find we can bridge the gap with the Victorians and acknowledge our shared predicament, one that is fully "modern."

This, then, is the spirit in which to approach someone like F. D. Maurice. It is a tribute to the coherence in Maurice's thinking that each of the following chapters turns on a common theme: division, strife, fragmentation, disunity. Richard Norris, who begins the study with a chapter on Maurice and theological method, takes as a point of departure Maurice's notorious dislike of sects, parties, and movements, of any set of opinions that excludes one group to include another. Frank McClain focuses on the disruption that expresses itself in inequalities between the sexes, and on Maurice's theological basis for advocating the equality of men and women created in the image of God. John Orens writes about Maurice and the life of prayer, the work of prayer in bringing human diversity and variance into communion with the whole race in Christ, as opposed to what Maurice called our efforts to "procure a separate pardon," to make a separate peace with God.

So the reason for this study, as I began saying, is not to indicate new directions in historical or feminist or ascetical theology. It is meant instead to convey something about F. D. Maurice and something about his vision of the kingdom of God, the ways in which this kingdom can be perceived and the ways it can be promoted. Perhaps the most important single thing Maurice has to teach us is not what the kingdom of Christ *is*, but how it is to be *found* — not how we are to establish it, but how we glimpse it, knock against it, come upon it by accident. Maurice never considered himself a "builder," but rather a "digger," an excavator of theological truths. Any study of his thought could do worse than to take for its text one of Matthew's parables of the Kingdom, where "the kingdom of heaven is like a treasure hidden in a field, which a man found and covered up; then in his joy he goes and sells all that he has and buys that field" (13:44). The kingdom of Christ, Maurice tells us, is already here, in the place where we come upon it. We don't have to establish it or build it or decree it, for the kingdom is enmeshed in the ties that bind us to one another and to heaven. And this argument is typical of Maurice, in the last analysis, for he would always want to relieve us of our burdens by reminding us of our responsibilities.

* * * * * * * * * * * * *

   This study began as a series of three lectures given at the Society of St. John the Evangelist during the month of October, 1981, for the benefit of community members, guests, and friends of the monastery. Accordingly I would like to thank Fr. Paul Wessinger, Superior, and the whole community for its sponsorship of the Cowley Lecture Series as well as for its hospitality to the lecturers themselves.

foreword

My thanks go also to Elizabeth Stouffer and John Orens for their help in preparing this manuscript for publication, to Jane Redmont for her willingness to photograph Lechmere on a cold day and so give the book its cover, and to Charles Hefling and Tuck Shattuck for their patience in reading and criticizing the foreword.

Cynthia Logan, Editor
Cowley Publications

[xvii]

MAURICE

ON

THEOLOGY

"In the last resort, then, 'system' in Maurice's thought is a term roughly equivalent in its force to the word 'idol' in the Hebrew Scriptures. It is the name of an illusory alternative to reality."

RICHARD NORRIS

The Church of England, and in its wake the other churches of the Anglican Communion, has tended to make something of a fetish of being religiously and theologically inclusive. Many labels have been employed to give expression to this singular characteristic. In the old days it was fashionable to speak of the Church of England as representing a *via media*, or as being a "bridge" church, because of the manner in which it embraced, even if it did not always contrive to reconcile, both the dogmas of the Reformation and the more "catholic" order, style, and piety of the patristic and mediaeval eras. More recently, this language has tended to disappear; instead one hears, in obvious despite of the Thirty-Nine Articles of Religion, that Anglicanism is "nonconfessional." Or else it is said that the churches springing from the English Reformation are "comprehensive," making room in their extraordinarily capacious laps not merely for Protestantism and Catholicism, but also for almost any species of liberalism or modernism. What is more, the passionless observer of the present state of Anglicanism would probably be compelled to agree with this claim.

Richard Norris

To agree that the claim is just, however, is by no means the same thing as to rejoice in the state of affairs to which it bears witness. Professor Stephen Sykes, in a troubling little book called *The Integrity of Anglicanism*, has taken it upon himself to deprecate the whole spirit of "comprehensiveness." He does this, clearly enough, not because he wishes to stop theological debate or to bind every teacher and preacher to a perfectly uniform pattern of doctrine, but, first of all, because he thinks that "the Anglican communion . . . has a standpoint on matters of doctrine," and, second, because he thinks that the ideal of comprehensiveness "has served as an open invitation to intellectual laziness and self-deception."[1] Comprehensiveness, in short, has become, in Sykes's opinion, an excuse for pretending that questions of truth in doctrine make no difference, and thus the excuse for a pervasive anti-theological bias.

What makes Sykes's argument interesting for our purposes, however, is not his general thesis, but rather the fact that he sees in the late Frederick Denison Maurice the principal source of what he calls the "bogus theory of comprehensiveness, which for far too long has lain like a fog over the Anglican mind." Maurice's theory, Sykes observes, is that "the Church of England has achieved not a middle course of compromise, but a union of opposites"; and this theory had its roots in Maurice's "well-known dislike for ecclesiastical parties."[2] Maurice in fact gives the impression of thinking that when two groups representing incompatible points of view find themselves in conflict, the truth which is at issue is somehow to be found, not with the one party or the other, but in a marriage of the two extremes. Maurice suggests, moreover, that the reason why principles which are in fact complementary are perceived as incompatible is that they get distorted in some fashion by being made

[4]

the basis of exclusive systems. Thus, as Sykes is quick to point out, Maurice's distaste for such phenomena as Puseyism or Evangelicalism stems from a distrust of what he calls "systems" — and hence, presumably, from a disinclination for the sort of careful, systematic thinking which Sykes desiderates for the theologian. Maurice is, then, not merely the author of a somewhat unrealistic view of the English Church, but the fount of an anti-intellectual, anti-theological current which has, in more recent times, inundated Anglicanism.

No one who has read even a small sampling of Maurice's voluminous writings can fail to recognize in Sykes's account certain characteristic themes in Maurice's thought. Certainly the polemic against "system" and "sect" and "party" looms very large indeed in his books and letters alike. It is turned, moreover, not only against ecclesiastical groups and movements, but against philosophical schools of thought and political and social theories. On the other hand, it is striking that this opponent of system and firm believer in the *complexio oppositorum* should have been perceived, both in his own time and by present-day interpreters, as the advocate and the originator of a theological system. Dr. Pusey, writing from his prophet's chamber at Christ Church, could speak with an obvious shudder of Maurice's "theology," which he prefers not to discuss.[3] Bishop Wilberforce of Oxford, though he judged that Maurice's *Theological Essays* contained "a great deal of obscurity," was nevertheless convinced that Maurice had in his other works declared himself "repeatedly" and comprehensibly — if idiosyncratically — on the principal topics of Christian doctrine.[4] These testimonies, which suggest that Maurice was hardly perceived in his own day as a noncommittal advocate of comprehensiveness, are confirmed by modern treatments of Maurice's thought. Dr. Torben Christensen has, indeed, taken the trouble to set out Maurice's systematic theology in one volume and made a more than merely plausible case for his contention that there is "coherence and consistency in Maurice's teaching"[5] — a teaching which Maurice, with his near-prophetic sense of vocation, envisaged as a radical criticism of the orthodoxies of his day.

We seem, then, to be presented with not one but two F. D. Maurices. On the one hand there is the opponent of "system," the prophet of comprehension and reconciliation — in a word, the friendly and somewhat fuzzy-minded Broad Churchman. On the other hand there is Maurice the polemicist, who has thought through the "sense" of the Christian message for himself, and has arrived at conclusions which appear to him, and to those of his contemporaries who can fathom his prose style, to be revolutionary in the proper sense of that word. In the absence, however, of clinical evidence that Maurice was a schizophrenic, one is bound to suspect that the hypothesis of two Maurices is unsatisfactory. Some inquiry must be made to determine just how a person with a relatively clear and coherent systematic position of his own could, nevertheless, be perceived, and want to be perceived, as the enemy of "system."

The question obviously is: what does Maurice take the enterprise of theology to be? And in order to get at an answer to that, we shall begin by examining his polemic against parties and systems in order, if possible, to tease out its presuppositions. It may be that, in the end, Maurice will turn out to have a contribution of his own to make to any contemporary discussion of the role of theological inquiry in the life of the Church.

§2

The best point at which to begin this investigation is in the opening sections of *The Kingdom of Christ,* where Maurice most clearly reveals his problem, his agenda, and his method. In the original preface which he wrote for the edition of 1838, Maurice announces the purpose of his work. It is to inquire whether there *is* a universal church, a "spiritual Kingdom." Careful note must be taken of the mood of his verb. He is not inquiring, or intending to inquire, whether there ought to be, or even whether, under certain circumstances, there might be, such a kingdom. His question is whether there *is* such a thing — whether humanity, will it or not, is as a matter of fact caught up in an all-embracing divine order.

No sooner, though, is this question posed, than Maurice must face two indubitable facts. The first is that the world is full of individuals and groups which possess and proclaim recipes for a universal order. The second is that these recipes are mutually inconsistent. The reality of his time and place was a series of parties, movements, and sects whose altercations not only dominated the life of Church and society, but also modulated every discussion of Maurice's theme into the key of blind controversy. This situation created a double problem for Maurice. On the one hand, its mere existence stood as evidence against the thesis he wanted to argue: that in fact there *is* a universal spiritual kingdom. On the other hand, every party, movement, and sect bore, in its own special way, testimony to a conviction that there is an order — an all-embracing order — which it is possible for the race to appropriate. The problem for Maurice, then, is how he shall assess this paradoxical state of affairs.

His response to the problem is as paradoxical as the problem itself. Maurice chooses to walk in two ways at once. His attitude appears in his observation that "what we want, is to be brought into a point of view, in which the fair and illuminated side of each [party's] doctrine, and not its dark side, may be presented to us."[6] The same point is made in other words when he writes: "We should be taught how to profit from the writings of men who have seen certain sides of the truth very strongly; how we may be prevented from rejecting what they rejected" (1:18). Maurice chooses, in short, to believe that in the creed of every party and movement there is some fundamental affirmation which must be taken seriously, and yet that at the same time every such creed has its "dark side." In his search for a universal spiritual kingdom, an order which embraces all of humanity and binds it in one, he will be at once the enemy and the ally of every party. Maurice will play the most thankless of roles — that of the friendly critic.

Needless to say, such a stance might easily amount to nothing more than the practice of a mindless (and merely conciliatory) eclecticism, which is the very error of which many of his contemporaries accused Maurice. The fact is, however, that this friendly criticism of his is invariably carried out in accordance with a strict hermeneutical principle. Maurice does not pick out here and there, from among the tenets of the various parties and schools, bits of teaching which appeal to him and, rejecting the rest, fashion his bits and pieces into some hybrid whole. On the contrary, he takes the curious view that the position of every contending group must be rejected and denied *as a whole* in as far as it assumes the shape of a "system"; it must at the same time be accepted and affirmed *as a whole* in as far as it represents what he likes to call a "principle."

[8]

There is, therefore, a remarkable consistency in Maurice's method of critical inquiry, although to understand it we must look more closely at the ideas which govern his procedures.

Consider, then, just as an example, the way in which Maurice deals with Quakerism in the opening chapter of *The Kingdom of Christ*. His first aim here is to describe what he calls "the positive doctrine of the Quakers" — which, we may assume, means "the fair and illuminated side" of their teaching. This positive doctrine he takes, not implausibly, to be the "principle of 'the light of Christ within' " (1:43) — the apprehension that there is "a light which lighteneth every man who cometh into the world." Maurice sees, moreover, that in this principle the Quakers have discerned and formulated the basis of "a dispensation which should have these two characteristics above all others — spirituality and universality" (1:46). The Quakers, in other words, are witnesses for the reality of the very order after which he, Maurice, is inquiring.

At the same time, their witness is flawed to the degree that they have identified their principle with, and thus embedded it in, a series of negations and denials. Because the light of Christ as they know and experience it is spiritual and interior, the Quakers denounce every kind of outward form or formula in religion. Even the Scriptures, which have testified to them of "the light of Christ within," they treat merely as an instrument (1:61). Thus Maurice writes,

A body asserting the positive doctrines, and having the negative characteristics I have described, gradually formed itself, and assumed to itself the name of *The Society of Friends*. This Society, its members believed, was called into existence to exhibit the features of that Kingdom which Christ came into the world to establish. Without wishing to be uncharitable, or denying that there might be good men who did not belong to it, yet they practically looked upon it as the Church of God on earth — the witness against the world. (1:61-62)

In this very act, however, Maurice goes on to say, Quakerism became a "system." This means that the mode of its presence in the world contradicts the very principle for which it stands and to which it is seeking to bear witness. Quakerism stands for a universal interior presence of the Christ to human persons, yet it bears its witness by isolating itself from a world it regards as impure. It has staked its identity on "indifference to outward badges" (1:69) in order to confess publicly the spiritual nature of the Kingdom of Christ, yet it has become dependent for its continuing existence on the maintenance of a new and distinctive set of external badges. In sum, the negations by which Quakerism has made of itself an exclusive system have caught it up in inconsistency and self-contradiction. Hence Maurice can insist that "far from thinking that the Quakers have carried their principles to an excess, I believe all their errors have arisen from the narrow, imperfect, and earthly notions which they entertain respecting the nature of a spiritual Kingdom" (1:58).

In this critical account of Quakerism, Maurice intimates very plainly the nature of his "friendly criticism." At first glance it is based, as we have seen, on a distinction between affirmations and negations. He wants to praise the Quakers — and for that matter the Protestants, the Roman Catholics, and the Utilitarians — for what they affirm, and to criticize them for the denials, the negations, by which they make of themselves a separated and exclusive body. This distinction, however, is correlated in Maurice's mind with another and somewhat more obscure contrast, which qualifies it significantly. When he speaks of a "positive doctrine" or affirmation, Maurice does not intend to signify just any statement of belief which is, or can be, couched in an affirmative sentence. He means, on the contrary, what he persistently calls "principles"; these in turn he distinguishes sharply from "notions," a term he has happily taken over from the Quakers themselves. Thus the affirmation of an inward light was for George Fox and his followers a "principle," while the doctrines about "justification, sanctification, final perseverance, and the like, which [Fox] had heard proclaimed from the pulpits of the day" were for him "mere notions."[7] For Maurice, then, the positive side of the teaching of any group consists in its *principles;* the negative side, in *notions.*

But then what is a principle, in Maurice's vocabulary? And what is there that is inherently negative about a notion? The first of these questions Maurice answers for us directly in his treatment of Quakerism itself. Referring again to George Fox, he writes: "The language of the preachers and of the books might be *about* something which concerned him and all men; but he had discovered the very thing itself; he had a fact to proclaim, not a theory or a system" (1:58). A principle, in other words, is a statement or expression which testifies directly of a reality, a state of affairs, and of the speaker's involvement with that reality. A notion, on the other hand, is in Maurice's vocabulary a statement or expression which is in the strictest sense secondary: it is an attempt to explain or to account for the reality to which a principle testifies. Thus in discussing what he calls "pure protestantism," Maurice can distinguish radically between justification as "a living thing...the deliverance of man's conscience from a burden and a bondage," and

[11]

justification as "a notion or theory about something which you call by this name" (1:111f). It is this latter sort of thing which Maurice associates with system, and which he sees as standing in almost inevitable conflict with the principle it seeks to explicate. He asks his readers, therefore, to take careful note

> how little the body which took justification by faith for its motto and principle, has been able, in any stage of its history, to assert that doctrine; how constantly the system, whether interpreted by earnest believers or stiff dogmatists, by orthodox doctors or mere moralists, has been laboring to strangle the principles to which it owes its existence. (1:115)

In the face of statements such as this, though, one is bound to pose our second question. Why is it that notions, systems, and opinions (all of which Maurice ties up in one parcel) stand against and contravene the very principles they are intended to explain and embody? Why, in short, does Maurice associate what he calls "system" with the negative factor in the position of every party or movement? Certainly there is no instantly obvious reason why he, or anyone else, should do so. A system of doctrine or opinion, after all, is no more than an attempt to elucidate some truth, to show it in all its connections and implications. Why, then, this hostility to system?

The answer to that question is nowhere stated and everywhere intimated in Maurice's writings; as one might expect in such circumstances, the answer is complex. The fact is that the term "system" — with its cousins "notion" and "opinion" — has, in Maurice's vocabulary, almost the richness of a symbol. It pulls together under a single label a whole spectrum of ideas and perceptions, and to understand his attitude towards systems one must

[12]

both disentangle its various senses and exhibit them in their relations to one another. Fortunately, there does seem to be a double theme or *leitmotiv* that runs through Maurice's various uses of the term. What characterizes a system for Maurice is first of all the fact that it excludes, that in one way or another it rives through the wholeness of things; second, that it is human creation as distinct from divine gift.

Thus, to begin with, "system" for Maurice is a correlative of "party" or "sect." The way in which one group distinguishes itself from another is precisely by its system; and therefore Maurice will speak of the "Evangelical, Liberal, Catholic, or purely Anglican" *systems* and describe them as "of the earth earthy," as carrying within them "the seeds of destruction."[8] It is system, then, which divides human beings and prevents them from having fellowship in the universal Kingdom of Christ. "I tremble to think," writes Maurice,

> what a crushing of all systems, religious and political, there must be, before we really do feel our gathering together in Christ to be the hope of the universe; before we acknowledge that the manifestation of the actual center of society, not the creation of some circle for ourselves or the indefinite enlargement of the circumference of our thoughts and notions, is what we should be looking for.[9]

Unlike principles, then, which point to realities which are given and given for *all*, systems are affairs of human devising whose effect — and indeed whose purpose — is to mark out boundaries, to divide and so to exclude. They aspire to universality, but are inevitably particularistic.

[13]

There is yet another sense in which, for Maurice, system excludes, and one which has nothing directly to do with the division of society by parties and sects. The fact is that systems distort reality and thus exclude whole ranges of truth from the scope of human knowledge and appreciation. The very attempt to grasp what is real within the confines of a single intellectual construction, however admirably and self-consistently it is wrought, induces blindness to everything the system cannot account for. Thus Maurice observes in his *Lectures on the Ecclesiastical History:*

> When once a man begins to build a system, the very gifts and qualities which might serve in the investigation of truth, become the greatest hindrance to it. He must make the different parts of the scheme fit into each other; his dexterity is shown, not in detecting facts, but in cutting them square.[10]

This does not mean, of course, that there is no truth, no intimation of reality, in the systems of thought which people construct for their comfort. Maurice affirms his conviction that even "fanaticism and...consciously dishonest quackery" are ineffective "unless they have some true principle to work with."[11] In every system there is a witness to the divine order which is the actual foundation of human existence. Nevertheless every system opposes the reality which it seeks to define, and does so precisely because it is not so much an attempt to enter into and appropriate that reality as an attempt to control it, to make things over in accordance with "arrangements of ours."[12] If systems do indeed exclude whole ranges of truth, then, at least one of the reasons why this is so is that they are an expression of human arrogance, of a desire to "frame a comprehensive system which shall include nature and society, man and God...and which therefore necessarily leads the system-builder to consider himself above them all."[13]

[14]

Systems, then, are human creations which divide humanity and distort reality — which exclude the "other" and at the same time exclude whole dimensions of truth. But in the last resort Maurice's most serious objection to systems, notions, and opinions is different from both of these. He phrases this objection most eloquently, perhaps, in a letter to Daniel Macmillan, his publisher, in 1844. In the letter Maurice observes:

> The one thought which possesses me most at this time and, I may say, has always possessed me, is that we have been dosing our people with religion when what they want is not this but the Living God. We are threatened now not with the loss of religious feelings, so-called, or of religious notions, or of religious observances, but with Atheism. Everywhere I seem to perceive this peril. That battle within, the battle without is against this; the heart and flesh of our countrymen are crying out for God. We give them a stone for bread, systems for realities.[14]

"Systems for realities" is the phrase that sums up Maurice's most fundamental judgment against what he calls systems, opinions, and notions. These become, in effect, a substitute for, and not merely a distortion of, reality. When J. M. Ludlow induced him to read James Anthony Froude's *Nemesis of Faith*, Maurice's reaction to the book brought him back to this same theme. The hero of Froude's book, he asserts in a letter of 1849, substituted a "religion *about* God" for "his belief *in* God," and in doing so exemplified what Maurice calls the heresy of the age, which turns out to be "religion against God."[15]

In both of these letters to Macmillan and to Ludlow, he equates religion with system and characterizes both as *substitutes* for reality. Maurice's contention is, apparently, that systems become in

[15]

practice the object of people's allegiance and faith: men and women devote themselves to causes, convictions, and beliefs rather than to what is properly the ground of every cause, the subject of every commitment, and the object of every belief. In the last resort, then, "system" in Maurice's thought is a term roughly equivalent in its force to the word "idol" in the Hebrew Scriptures. It is the name of an illusory alternative to reality.

§3

What are we to conclude from this survey of Maurice's polemic against systems, notions, and opinions? Does he in fact reveal himself to be anti-theological — an advocate of cheerful fuzzy-mindedness in doctrinal discourse? Or shall we say instead that his polemic points to a theological program, and hints at a theological method?

One thing at any rate is clear. Maurice was, as his first biographer and all his later interpreters have insisted, an apostle of unity. The first and most obvious note, therefore, in his polemic against system is Maurice's objection to its divisive character. System is a way of taking what is universal and making it over into something special and private. It turns principles which declare the truth about all persons into notions which are the peculiar property of this group or that group. In this way it not only falsifies them, but also makes them subjects of needless contention and controversy. Hence the fundamental object of what we have called Maurice's "friendly criticism" is to *set principles free from systems:* to engage in what is, at one level, a sheerly destructive hermeneutic. It is one which shall disentangle and liberate from every body of doctrine, every set of opinions and notions, those elements which declare, not the truth for this or that group, but the condition of humanity in Christ. One aim of his writing, therefore, is to be a witness for the unity, not of Christians merely, but of human beings in Christ.

To say this, however, is to state only half a truth, and to risk leaving a thoroughly false impression of the shape of Maurice's thought. For Maurice is no mild irenicist, busily trying to affirm whatever he can in everyone's position. No more is he suggesting that theological truth is found in a *complexio oppositorum,* since in his estimation opposing systems cannot be reconciled and different principles do not need to be reconciled. Nor, as far as I can see, does Maurice for one minute suppose that his account of the positive sense of the various systems he considers will be accepted by the ordinary representatives of those systems.

On the contrary, he understands himself to be saying something fundamentally offensive to the spirit of the orthodoxies of his age. Maurice affirms that there is a divine order, an established and given relationship of God and humanity, which subsists in, beyond, and in spite of human systems of all sorts. The task of theology, therefore, is not in his view that of pulling things together for the sake of unity. Rather it is that of uncovering a unity which is already given. Maurice wants to be like the apostle Paul, who, to "the ignorant, idolatrous inhabitants of Athens," announces not as a theory but as a fact, "for in Him we live and move and have our being."[16]

There is, then, in Maurice's thought, a principle which transcends and undergirds his search for unity. It is the principle that the task of theology is a task not of construction, but of discovery. He expresses this idea in a number of ways. To one of these we have alluded already; it consists in the very phraseology of the question which his work *The Kingdom of Christ* addresses: "Is there a Catholic Church?" Maurice understands himself — no doubt surprisingly — to be asking a question of fact. Similarly, Maurice understands his role as a cleric and a theologian to be that of "proclaiming society and humanity to be divine realities." Again he writes, "To preach the Gospel of [the] Kingdom, the fact that it is among us, and is not to be set up at all, is my calling and business."[17]

The conviction which consumes Maurice is not that of the need for unity. It is that of the reality of God and of the givenness of a "constitution" of humanity in Christ. Consequently when Maurice talks of theology, he does so in deliberately provocative terms, insisting that theology is "the knowledge of God and not the teaching of a religion." It is because of this that he can assert, "My business, because I am a theologian, and have no vocation except for theology, is not to build but to dig, to show . . . that society . . . is to be regenerated by finding the law and ground of its order in God."[18] In other words, the theologian is not an inventor of systems intended to meet or to justify religious needs, but an inquirer into the ultimate basis of all human activity and life: God.

> Theology is not (as the schoolmen have represented it) the climax of all studies, the Corinthian capital of a magnificent edifice . . . ,

[18]

but is the foundation upon which they all stand. And even that language would have left my meaning open to a very great... misunderstanding, unless I could exchange the name theology for the name God, and say that he himself is the root from which all human life, and human society, and ultimately, through man, nature itself, are derived.[19]

It must therefore be plain that in the last resort Maurice's polemic against systems is inspired, not solely by his sense of the divisiveness which they produce, but even more by his sense that they distort and conceal reality and so become a substitute for it. What in the end he opposes is the notion that the theologian is in the business of constructing a reality within which people can live — whether that reality turns out to be a merely mental "world" or takes shape outwardly in some particularistic and exclusive society. The theologian is dealing with an ultimate mystery which is known through the testimony of a particular history and a particular movement within history. That mystery, however, is no one's special property. What the Scriptures and the ordered life and worship of the Church testify to is a universal order which embraces all of humanity in all of its concerns. Hence the business of the theologian is to trace, painstakingly, the contours of that reality, and not to build it or to make it up. What such a tracing might be, and how it might be carried on, Maurice attempts to show in his own work. It consists not in the building of systems, but in the criticism of them; this means in turn an attentive search for the living principles to which systems bear witness even as they distort them. Theology is the attempt to uncover the foundation of human existence.

§4

Needless to say, acceptance of this programme does not involve any anti-theological bias. In his strictures against system, Maurice is not advocating vagueness or intellectual irresponsibility. His aim, rather, is to warn every theologian that the subject of theological discourse is not theology but God, and humanity's relation to God. Since, however, God is by hypothesis a reality universal in scope, all theological utterance must seek in principle to speak what is true of and for all people in their common relation to God. No doubt this canon is calculated to inspire the theologian with a certain spirit of modesty; modesty is not the same thing as vagueness or intellectual irresponsibility. On the contrary, modesty springs out of a methodical self-discipline — a willingness to correct and to be corrected in the face of a reality which is what it is, and not necessarily what theologians think it probably ought to be.

On the other hand, there are kinds of theological enterprise which Maurice's principles would in fact discourage. He would not, for example, care to have a hand in any attempt to define a normative Anglicanism: Anglicanism, as he understands it, is a system. No doubt one might try to offer an historical description of the sort of thing Anglicanism has tended to be, and one might find the resulting account to be entirely engaging and attractive. The theologian, however, can only look upon Anglicanism with a critical eye and ask what, in this historical phenomenon, stands as valid testimony to the reality of the one God who in Christ has constituted humanity as the recipient of grace and the subject of election. Such an inquiry will very likely fail to produce evidence that Anglicans possess any special virtue besides that of being members of Christ, children of God, and inheritors of the kingdom of heaven. Maurice would think that quite enough to say and it is hard, in the end, to disagree with him.

MAURICE

ON

WOMEN

"It is one of the distinctive functions of women to be ministers and witnesses of wholeness, of that unity which reflects the community of equals."

FRANK McCLAIN

I t is always important to be aware of a veritable pitfall in the path of anyone who tries to interpret Maurice. There is an opaque and confusing quality to his style which, albeit set off by epigrammatic jewels of light, tends to allow readers to project their own thoughts onto Maurice's mind. Certainly it is a point of which to be wary, but this weakness may be forgiven. Was not the prophet who prophesied into his waist-coat pocket himself the master of what some wag has labeled the "conjectorial assumptive"?

§

"You are so proud, Mr. Maurice, that you would not be seen with me in public!" exclaimed Miss Kemble to a young man then in his twenty-first year. "If you go down Regent Street on an elephant," the youth retorted, "I will ride beside you on a donkey!"[1]

This to a lady whose "Juliet" would electrify London in 1829, and whose American divorce scandalized the world in 1848. Frederick Denison Maurice was the young man. His familiarity and ease with Fanny Kemble, that passionate Victorian, was indicative of the relationship he shared with many, if not most, of those impressive women who in the nineteenth century were involved in what our present day calls the feminist movement. His contemporary female colleagues, as well as his students, rank as leaders in that age which marked the greatest advancement in the position of women that the world had yet seen. English-speaking women's education owed its very quality, as well as its form and structure, to two among Maurice's first half-dozen pupils at Queen's College, Harley Street.

> Miss Buss and Miss Beale, love's darts do not feel!
> How different from us, Miss Beale and Miss Buss!

are words which every English schoolgirl knows. They never let us forget the work of Dorothea Beale (1831-1906) and Frances Mary Buss (1827-1894), Maurice's first students. Cheltenham Ladies' College is a more tangible monument to Miss Beale than poetry, for it has set the standards for the educated English woman. Miss Buss's North London Collegiate School and Bedford College of the University of London equally attest the vitality with which Maurice imbued the young women who carried on his ideas.

Octavia Hill (1838-1912), whose mature work is more often related to her association with John Ruskin, was another of those women whom Maurice guided into their life's work. Emily, Octavia's younger sister, married Maurice's son Edmund; Octavia, who never married, may well be called the mother of urban renewal. Following her association with Maurice in the Working

Women's College, Miss Hill hit upon the scheme of buying, restoring, and leasing to the poor a great many residential buildings in the poorest sections of London. More importantly, Octavia Hill involved herself directly with the tenants; the personal influence of the "social worker," she thought, was the most important factor in human rehabilitation. Indefatigable, Miss Hill has another witness in our day in the National Trust, which preserves a heritage of beauty in Britain and gives a model internationally for the preservation of open spaces.

The sisters Winkworth, Susanna (1820-1884) and Catherine (1827-1878), are perhaps best known to Americans for their contributions to American hymnody. However in 1868 together with Maurice they formed a center for the Committee for the Higher Education of Women. Jenny Lind (1820-1887), whose financial support of Maurice was always generous, worked faithfully with the Winkworth sisters, and Harriet Martineau (1820-1910) was another associate — although she and Maurice were never friends, and more than once he refused her overtures for cooperation between them. Another of Maurice's colleagues was Mrs. Gaskell (Elizabeth Cleghorn Gaskell, 1810-1865), the friend and biographer of Charlotte Brontë. Her novel, *Ruth*, published in 1853, includes Frederick Maurice as a principal figure, a clergyman who brings gentleness and strength into women's shattered lives. Maurice read and specifically acknowledged his debt to many of the women for whom authorship provided the only direct avenue to financial independence.

Barbara Leigh-Smith, Mme. Bodichon (1827-1891), was instrumental in the passage of the Married Women's Property Act with her *Brief Summary of the Laws Concerning Women*. It was

[27]

Mme. Bodichon who, with Maurice's young friend Emily Davies (1830-1921), founded Girton College and brought women finally to acceptance at the University of Cambridge. Maurice's debt to another colleague, Mrs. Jameson (Anna Brownell Jameson, 1794-1860), is incalculable. Works such as *Characteristics of Shakespeare's Women* (dedicated to Fanny Kemble), *Relative Social Position of Mothers and Governesses,* and *Female School of Art* left an indelible mark on him. Another strong influence on Maurice was Josephine Butler's *Women's Work and Women's Culture,* and *On the Education and Employment of Women,* which are reflected directly in Maurice's *Social Morality.* Mrs. Butler (1828-1906) is also remembered for her efforts to repeal the Contagious Diseases Acts in 1870, acts which provided for the registration and compulsory medical examination of prostitutes, thereby extending an unofficial sanction to the practice of prostitution itself.

Over and over again in Maurice we hear echoes of Mary Wollstonecraft (1759-1797), whose words Maurice would have heard repeated in the voice of his mother. The *Vindication of the Rights of Women* (1792) confirmed Maurice's view that woman "seems born to teach and practice physic; to restore health to the sick and to preserve it to the well," and Wollstonecraft's attack on Rousseau's opposition to women's education was a watch cry for Maurice. "The more they resemble our sex the less power will they have over us," exclaimed the philosopher. "This is the very point I am at: I do not wish them to have power over men but over themselves," was Mrs. Wollstonecraft's reply.[2]

Power over themselves! Power to be women! What could these words mean at a time when women were at best merely playthings, and at worst simply the possessions and chattel of the male half of the population. In its discussion of the feminine advance from dependence and subordination, so much a part of the history of women, the *Encyclopedia Brittanica* records: "The conviction that it was neither good nor politic for women to remain in their former state of ignorance was gradually accepted by everyone. The movement owed much to Frederick Denison Maurice. He was its pioneer."[3]

It has sometimes been wondered why Frederick Denison Maurice failed to be set amongst that distinguished number of *Eminent Victorians* in Lytton Strachey's study of those giants conscious of their present prestige and confident of their future power. After all, Maurice had taken Strachey's uncle Edward as a private pupil and he might well have attracted the interest of that iconoclastic biographer. Nevertheless in the comfortable respectability of nineteenth-century England, no one stood out more clearly as looking beneath the apparently untroubled surface of the age and questioning that society than this Victorian with a difference. Olive Brose, in her distinguished analysis of Maurice's theological stance, refers to him as the *Rebellious Conformist*. According to Mrs. Brose, two incompatabilities lie close together in Maurice's mind: a monumental conservatism which sees the institutions of the family, the nation, and the church as divine, coupled with a truly radical faith in the person of Jesus Christ.

Olive Brose speaks of Maurice's "quite unique concept of man-as-Image as the fundamental relation between God and man."[4] Nowhere does the tension between Maurice's radical faith, his unique understanding of man as the image of God, and his social conservatism emerge more clearly than in his deep concern for the feminine cause. As a theologian and as an author, Maurice brought a new vision to what it means to be a woman. Members of the one family of God, women share equal rights with all other children of the same parent. In the creation story of Genesis God had said, "Let us make man in our image, after our likeness. . . . So God created man in his own image, in the image of God created he him; male and female created he them." Women, though different from men, are yet integral and complementary parts of a whole. Along with the male, the female stands conjointly in the position of man-as-Image of God.

For Maurice, whose Unitarian heritage was balanced by a profound Trinitarian conviction, the divine nature reveals itself through Holy Scripture, through history, through reason, and through experience, as a community of persons. He acknowledges the Trinity, Father, Son, and Holy Spirit, "neither confounding the Persons: nor dividing the Substance," in the words of the Athanasian Creed. Intimacy within the being of God, in unity of substance yet without confusion of persons, Maurice believes to be reflected above all in human relationships. The fundamental relation between God and man informs relationships particularly between members of a family, husbands and wives, parents and children, brothers and sisters. These very relationships, Maurice asserts, are the pathway to the knowledge of God: "They are not artificial types of something divine, but are actually the means, and the only means through which man ascends to any knowledge of the divine."[5] The primal relationship between male and female is not only of divine origin, it is itself the paradigmatic relationship which helps to illuminate all others.

Maurice's loyalty to women was not so much a matter of development from one stage to another. The position which allowed him as a twenty-year-old to condemn current ladies' studies as "malicious and perverse," for destroying what nature "designed to be the best and most glorious part of creation," and the hope of his old age that "the tone of young women's thoughts about themselves and their relations with men be raised," is one and the same.[6] From the beginning until the end of his life, Maurice's relationships with women as members of his family, instructors and counselors, colleagues and friends, shows an unwavering loyalty to a vision of humanity as a whole, reflecting the unity within the being of God, joined like heaven and earth in one race in the person of Jesus Christ as the Head, in whom male and female are one.

§2

How did Maurice's concern for women's rights and the position of women in society arise? What were the specific forms that it took, and what were the practical results of his efforts? Finally, in what way are we able to find Maurice's thoughts about the nature of women (he would have hated the abstraction "feminine") helpful to us today, when Victorian battles often seem only a dim memory of a distant age?

We need look no farther than the household in which Maurice was born and in which he grew to manhood to discern how Maurice's concern for women arose. The role of his mother and, particularly, his sisters cannot be overestimated. There were eight of these sisters in the family, none of them of a retiring disposition. Almost as far back as the young boy could remember, conflict over questions of religious faith shattered the domestic life of the Maurices. One by one the sisters abandoned the Unitarian chapel of which their father, Michael Maurice, was the minister. Even Mrs. Maurice herself found that she was unable to worship in the congregation served by her husband. The women of the family would characteristically arise from the breakfast table, closet themselves, and write long explanatory letters to one another, defending their personal religious convictions and attacking the beliefs of the others.

One venture drew sisters and mother together. Shortly after the family had moved from Norfolk to the village of Frenchay near Bristol, the indomitable Misses Maurice established classes; women came regularly to the Maurices' house to be instructed in the simple fundamentals of literacy. They were divided into groups according to their previous instruction and present abilities. Then in his tenth year, young Frederick, the future educator of women, described the meetings to a friend. Maurice's first piece of recorded authorship, a bit of childhood doggerel, deals with the interest of women in education.

> Oh Jones! How I wish that with equal discerning
> The *men* like the *women* were lovers of learning!
> That "the ladies are given to change" poets say:
> But, as you my dear friend the remark won't betray
> In justice to them I must own in this letter
> That when they do change t's a change for the better.
> A better example I scarcely can mention,

[32]

Or give better proof of the female attention,
For though twenty-two came the Sunday before
O' would you believe it they're now 44.
  . . .
These women I doubt not are anxious to learn
That when to their husbands at home they return
They sharply may say while he looks like a fool,
'I am better than you, Sir! for I've been to school.'
Well! Whilst in our study the wives make a riot
One hour in the week the poor men are in quiet,
Lamenting the troubles on wedlock that fall,
And advising their sons not to marry at all.7

The emotional atmosphere of the Maurice household was,
then, quite obviously highly charged. Religious controversy often
indicates a more subtle imbalance in a community, and this must
certainly have been the case in a family of women where personal
tensions were increasingly strong between the sisters. The young
Frederick Maurice could not help but be marked by the power of
the feminine which surrounded his infancy and boyhood.

The first and most important influence upon his emerging
psychological consciousness came from his mother, Priscilla Hurry
Maurice. The bond between the two was heightened by the loss,
shortly before Frederick's birth, of another son. The ensuing closeness between them allowed Maurice to be particularly open with
his mother, and it stimulated a ready interchange of ideas between
them. Concerned more often than not about her health, and believing herself on one occasion to be dying, Mrs. Maurice not in-
frequently fell into despair about the future as well as the present
state of her eternal soul. Her son functioned as a strong supportive
presence in all these trials, and this habit of nurturing women was

to be one of the distinctive characteristics of his life.

But he received much from his mother as well as gave. "My mother," Maurice writes in a letter, had "a far clearer intellect than my father, a much more lively imagination, a capacity for interests in a number of subjects, and an intense individual sympathy."

> I do think there was in me a love of truth for its own sake which has kept alive in me ever since. . . . I am sure my mother's own sincerity cultivated that love much more; and if my father had any hope of making me business like and scientific, he certainly failed.[8]

Mrs. Maurice's use of such terms as "principles," "everlasting," "eternal life," are quite as unlike the conventional use of her day as her son's use of them was unlike the conventional use of his time. In fact, Mrs. Maurice's letters could be regarded as the dictionary of her son's writings. Maurice always acknowledged that in this, as well as in other respects, he had received more from women than from men in the shaping of his life's work. Such clarity of intellect and liveliness of imagination as he received from his mother was a positive strength.

Needless to say, however, the spiritual malaise of the household took its toll. The young Maurice himself fell into the deep states of depression which were to characterize his later life. The cause of these depressions can be traced to the influence of women, but, at the same time, it was a woman who first came to his rescue. It is to an unknown figure, "dear Lucy," that we must be grateful in large measure for the early development of Maurice's eventual and positive religious affirmation. At the age of sixteen, and apparently having accepted the rigid Calvinist dogmatism adopted by his mother and sisters, Maurice wrote to this woman and described himself as "a being destined to a few short years of misery here, as an earnest of and preparation for that more enduring state of wretchedness and woe. . . ." In reply, she wrote to pose this question: "What is your authority for regarding any individual of the human race as *destined* to misery either here or hereafter?"[9] His present state of feelings must be due to God's love, she went on to say, and a step forward, not downward. In thinking about this, it is useful to remember Maurice's later affirmation that we can never have a consciousness of separation and sin unless we have a consciousness of God. It is God who places the consciousness in our hearts. We can only acknowledge separation, a broken state, if we have a previous intimation of what it is to be whole.

Maurice's special friendship with his sister Emma was another impetus leading him toward religious maturity. He had completed his work at Cambridge in 1826, taking a First Class in Law. Unwilling to subscribe to the Thirty-Nine Articles, a requirement for taking the Cambridge degree, Maurice had gone down from the University without it and had entered upon the life of a young intellectual in London, writing for literary journals and later editing the *Athenaeum.* Haunted by a sense of incompleteness, Maurice returned to academic study at Oxford, where subscription to the Articles was a prerequisite for admission. Subscribing to the Articles in 1829, and embarking on a course of study at Exeter College, Oxford, which would prepare him for ordination, Maurice was still troubled.

He poured out his confusion to his sister Emma, who was the sister nearest in age and temperament to his own. They had been especially close when they were children in the nursery, a closeness made more intense now when Emma, on her death bed, was gradually becoming weaker and weaker. Maurice, at the time, was absorbed in writing his novel *Eustace Conway* and planned to finance his academic studies by the proceeds of his authorship. The book concerns itself with the psychological development, intellectual maturity, and religious faith of a young man very like himself. It was an important time in his life and his conversations with his sister were crucial. He remembers her as singularly wise, bearing with his incoherencies and depressions. "It astonishes me now," he recorded, "what a method she took to cure me of them." "She encouraged me to complete [the novel]. . . . Scarcely anyone but one so good as she was could have discovered any good in it but she did. She believed that I was trying to say something that it was better for me to say, and that I should see my path more clearly if I did."[10] The novel, completed in three volumes, is an important statement of Maurice's belief. Few, if any, of his later, mature ideas are not found, at least in embryo, in the youthful work.

Maurice also acknowledged his indebtedness to his older sister, Elizabeth. Far too little attention has been paid to this interesting and probably psychologically unbalanced woman. Jilted in love and subject to seizures, Elizabeth had eventually come under the healing influence of an Anglican clergyman and it was she who was first among the Maurices to become a member of the Church of England. After Emma's death in 1831, the struggle between the intense pietism of his family and other conflicting feelings continued to produce such internal stress that Maurice was plunged regularly and even more deeply into fits of depression. His sister Elizabeth showed him an

> eager sympathy, giving him courage to trust in lessons which as
> he believed he was learning from a higher tutor, than anything

very original in her, is the important element.... Seeing that pietism for him embodied itself in his sister Emma, it will not be difficult to realize how much he needed among those who loved and revered her as he did some one who should press him forward."[11]

It was Elizabeth who urged and led her brother on his spiritual quest. She introduced him not only to the Anglican expression of the Catholic faith, but also to the views of the Reverend James Stephenson, under whom Maurice served his title as curate. Stephenson's millenarian beliefs were transformed by the young Maurice into his most distinctive idea, the belief in an underlying, although invisible, order of human relationships which was established by Jesus of Nazareth in his life, death, and resurrection. Maurice affirms this order in *The Kingdom of Christ*, his first and unquestionably greatest work of theology. There exists beneath all visible societies, even when they do not conform to the divine order, a harmony of relationships which need only to be acknowledged and obeyed. Obedience to the kingship of Christ brings about its full realization.

If it was Elizabeth who enabled her brother to articulate some of his most important ideas, it was Maurice's sister Mary who worked most closely with her brother throughout his life and enabled him, perhaps even stung him, to put his beliefs into positive action. Mary deserves her own careful study among Victorian women. Entirely practical and business-like, it was she to whom her mother gave charge of her younger sisters when Mrs. Maurice thought herself to be dying. In 1829 at a time of family financial disaster, Mary Maurice responded to the crisis by establishing a school for children. She ranks as one of the earliest educators who studied and applied Pestalozzian methods to infant education; such methods, even today, are the foundation of the principles of children's kindergartens. In a period of happier financial fortunes, as we shall see, it was with Mary that Maurice worked most closely in setting up the Governesses' Benevolent Institution. She provided as well the driving force in the creation of the governesses' hospital and, after that, the establishment of the college for women in Harley Street. She never gave up practical projects as long as she lived and her work in establishing lifeboat rescue societies was commemorated by public subscription in Lowestoft, a monument destroyed by enemy action in the 1940's.

The happiest, and certainly the most wholesome of Maurice's relationships, his marriage to his first wife stands out as a splendid example of the interdependence of masculine and feminine. It is illustrative, too, of one principle of this intercharge that some have put forward. Just as a man brings forth creative action out of his feminine nature, so the inner masculine side of a woman brings forth creative seeds to fertilize the feminine side of the man. This principle was certainly at work in the marriage of Frederick Maurice and Annie Barton. Unfortunately the marriage lasted only seven years, from 1837 until Annie Maurice's death in 1845. We have an intriguing picture of the everyday events of their household in which Maurice is reputed to have dictated *The Kingdom of Christ* to his wife while he strode back and forth across the room, hugging a hard black horsehair cushion to his breast, and compulsively thrusting a red hot poker into the glowing coals of the fire. Annie Barton was beyond doubt an intellectual stimulus to her husband. She knew German, and it is certain that it was she who first read Schleiermacher to him. Not only astute, she possessed a wit that stands out as one of the few enlivening qualities of Maurice's domestic history. Annie Barton was at first reluctant to marry Maurice. A letter written after she accepted his proposal explains somewhat this reluctance, revealing that she has been "haunted by the feeling that it was not me but an ideal of your own to which you had given my name and to whom you were really attached."[12]

If Maurice finds human relationships the key to the divine nature of God, it is in the fundamental relationship of marriage that he sees most clearly that union of opposites, male and female, masculine and feminine, which provides the dynamic energy of creation. In the marriage relationship, more than anywhere else, is the nature of woman clearly perceived: feminine and masculine are equal, the union of opposites into one complete whole.

Maurice's first understanding of marriage appears in the final passage of his one novel, published not long before he met Annie Barton. After the novel's account of seemingly interminable trials which beset the hero, it finally achieves a resolution in which its hero, Eustace Conway, is addressed thus:

> You have hitherto to buffet with your enemies alone: it was with yourself you were fighting, and what friend could be a witness or a partaker of that conflict? But in all the disappointments of your future warfare, in all its triumph, you will have one to sympathize with you, one to warn you when you are strong, one to help you when you are weak, — one who will think with you, hope with you, fear with you, love with you, — a counsellor, a friend, a wife.[13]

The principle of the union of the sexes which marriage expresses is a unity of opposites. Differences between the sexes, differences between the persons, have to be discovered and acknowledged and affirmed before there can be that wholeness in which both members of the union can realize their own individual integrity. A husband, says Maurice, should never attempt to shape a wife in accordance with a pattern of his own. It is imperative, rather, that a man marry "a living creature whom God has formed and believe that he has managed the matter more wisely than any of his wise servants could."[14]

Maurice in speaking of marriage often refers to the scriptures of the Old Testament, and writes in *Social Morality* that "it is on the conjugal relation that the mind of the prophet most constantly dwells." How horrible in marriage to find inequality:

> The relation of the man and woman which is expressed in marriage, the dependence of each upon the other, is lost in the attempt to exalt either at the expense of the other. Separate them that you may glorify the strength of the man or the tenderness of the woman, — the strength and the tenderness depart, either because the strength becomes brutal and the tenderness imbecility, or because the strength apes the tenderness and the tenderness the strength.[15]

Examples of such confusion, which result from the exaltation of one sex over the other, are apparent in the mediaeval tradition of courtly love. The reverence and, indeed, worship of women there, Maurice senses, had been a natural counteraction of the Muhammadan tendency to degrade women. Inevitably, however, the exaltation of the woman led to abuses: "As the superiority of the sex was asserted, its dignity was undermined."[16]

A greater evil was compounded, however, by a degradation of women to the position of chattel. Maurice more than once compares the shameful position of women with the institution of slavery in the American states. In the case of slavery, the master is as much degraded as the slave: "Domestic life must subdue slavery or be subdued by it."[17] Husbands and wives are in a similar situation. The same principle, open and active dependence upon one another, trust, the ethos of the *"conjugium,"* must inform all the relationships of society, economic affairs, and social interchange. Destroy the one relationship and every relationship is damaged. The quality of trust, each person giving willingly and receiving what is needed from the other, best defines every relationship between men and women, the single as well as the married. The quality of the *"conjugium"* is ideally mirrored in simple and ordinary friendships between the sexes. Single men and women are at their best where reverence for one another is uppermost in the relationship, a willingness to give and receive freely. Maurice's friendships with women, especially those with single women, are good examples of such friendships between the sexes.

He develops his belief in the mutual interdependence of the sexes in an astonishing article which appeared in 1863 in the first issue of Emily Faithfull's *Victoria Magazine.* Miss Faithfull, later Printer to the Queen, had established a publishing company which employed only women, and she approached Maurice about the controversial subject of the newly-established religious orders for women in the Church of England. In the article he wrote, "On Sisterhoods," Maurice develops a rather puzzling thesis which supports the new foundations — in as much as they emphasize the *dependence* of the sexes upon one another! "Never the man without the woman, not the woman without the man."[18]

Maurice's understanding of women and of the feminine was, accordingly, nourished by what he received in early life from his mother, his sisters, and his wife. These early relationships and experiences also prepared him for what he was later to contribute to the cause of women's rights in his time.

§3

Beginning in 1826, his twenty-first year and the year before he was to go down from Cambridge, Maurice wrote a series of articles on education in general, and on women's education in particular.[19] A proper education would be in his opinion lifelong, but Maurice also stresses the fact that this education must begin at the breast. Sensual, intellectual, and religious faculties do not spring up by chance. There is an order in the development of the faculties; instruction must take place at the right time. It is hopeless, Maurice argues, to expect sound infant education from mothers whose business is coquetry. This is a sorely-needed lesson for Englishmen, he goes on to assert, upon whom lies the disgrace of the bad education which has crippled the powers, and destroyed the utility, of that sex which God and nature had intended to be the instructors and counselors of the male.

Thus Maurice challenges the prevailing attitude of the early nineteenth century and an educational process by which, he thinks, the female spirit has been "dragged down to earth and deprived of its native elasticity." For few young girls were actually taught at all; illiteracy was general. Lists of names and dates and facts provided the bulk of whatever instruction did take place. Teachers of schoolgirls showed a positive hatred for the intellectual part of every study, and preferred the technical and mechanical part. There appeared to be a desire to crush the intellect and destroy the imagination. Women were felt to be incapable of so much labor in education; their minds were said to be less vigorous. If that is so, exclaims Maurice the young educator, surely an education is best which counteracts a weakness. Should not an education cultivate the imagination as the most efficient auxiliary of the intellect?

Nothing, says Maurice, is so hard a labor as the use of memory in studying facts and forms. The books put into women's hands were by far the worst written, and they were made to learn them by heart. Maurice scorns the study of botany, which at that time was considered the only science suitable for females. In his day, the science of botany emphasized lists of things rather than principles, and oppressed the memory with particulars. Far better, he thinks, for women to become astronomers.

An incredible amount of time was also to be spent in the acquisition of so-called "accomplishments." Consider the six or seven hours a day to be spent in practicing the piano! Surely this was a pattern by which girls were being molded into ornaments or worse, into playthings, Maurice claims, through "studies most likely to make them find favour in the eyes of the Lords of Creation." On the contrary, a woman, once she gets beyond a position of subservience to a man, can begin to relate to him in a much more satisfying way for both; that is, as an equal. It is not through renouncing their sex, but by fulfilling it, that women will find themselves — by becoming true women, and not just bad imitations of men. It should be the desire and ambition of women not to assimilate them-

[43]

selves to men, or, for that matter, to separate themselves.

Writing in an article for *Macmillan's Magazine* in 1860, Maurice acknowledges his debt to the contemporary educator, Mrs. Jameson, with the words, "Women wished to be considered in all the relations, all the conditions of life, domestic and social as the *helpmate . . .*, not to be separated from men, but to be allowed to be nearer to them." Women are to be considered not as an appendage or garnish, but "as a part of [a man's] *life*, and all that is implied in the real sense of the word." Maurice goes on to say in this article, "As I am sure men have no reason to fear women as their rivals, so I hope women will, in all noble studies, be allowed henceforth to be their associates and companions."[20]

"We can only imagine a state of things in the reverse of the present," Maurice quips, "and we have an ideal of a system of female education." The exclusion of women, and the failure of women's education, not only deprives women themselves, but is a positive damage to society, specifically a damage to men. Every circle of men from which women are excluded supposes a certain number of women separated from them, and "the evil spirit of separation is far more fatal to those in whom it dwells than to those whom it tempts them to revile."[21]

The final and most individious consequence of the normal neglect of women's education is to be discovered in what Maurice thinks to be the "material, sensual, uncontemplative character of the religion of most pious women." In a series of lectures delivered by Maurice, Charles Kingsley, and others at Queen's College, London, Maurice brings up what is for him the greatest peril of this sort to the female mind. "The female mind," Maurice says there, "especially, if through desire of guidance it yields for awhile to decrees, soon creates some image for itself to worship." Females, he goes on to say, have "been most unfairly robbed of their precious culture," and "culture" he defines as the powers which are theirs as created in the image of God. Therefore Maurice holds that women are exposed more than most to charges of sophistry and Latitudinarianism. He fears that what is "deepest and most precious" in the female mind will not have been plumbed, and the result of this will be that women are liable to become "frivolous in their daily occupations — frivolous in their literature — frivolous in their science — frivolous in their religion."[22]

But this frivolity Maurice sees as an imminent danger, not as a present fact. In another context he locates "the choicest part of the religion of this country" among the female half of the population, citing their greater powers of faith, love, and self-denial. Maurice makes here a distinction, and one clearly important to him, between the different sorts of "cultivation" of the male and female mind; the latter cultivation he finds the nobler of the two. Women cultivate "the feelings which embrace and comprehend truth," Maurice writes, "[and] we the understandings which were destined to supply us with the outward and visible expressions of it. Our faculty is worth nothing without theirs." The distinction is between feelings and understandings, between truth and its outer trappings, which for Maurice is emblematic of the kinds of differences he sees between male and female. Perhaps that is also why Maurice claims that women cannot be theologians: "There probably does not exist a female in England who, in any proper sense of the word, can be said to possess a knowledge of theology..., merely an edifying proof that women, unless it shall be thought

[45]

expedient to give them a scientific education, never can become theologians."[23]

At the same time, Maurice did not think this dearth of theological knowledge was an inescapable factor, or a given of the female mind. His correspondence on theological matters with Samuel Taylor Coleridge's daughter, Sara, is an indication of how much he valued sharing the theological enterprise with a female mind. These letters often run thirty or forty pages in length. The Coleridge correspondence, which goes into the question of baptismal regeneration, comes as near to a systematic theology of the religious experience as Maurice, the theological "digger," ever achieved.[24]

§4

Eighteen-forty-eight, the year of revolution, saw the fruition of two specific and practical efforts for the improvement of the lot of women. Along with his sister Mary, and under the patronage of Lady Canning, Maurice and his companions were able to establish the Governesses' Benevolent Association. At that time, abject poverty faced the typical governess, too old or too sick to continue her employment. Three immediate aims were uppermost in the minds of the founders: to afford temporary relief in specific cases of great suffering, to encourage and make possible provident habits for those women who were able to save out of their all too often meager incomes, and to raise annuities for those women who were past work and whose friends and employers were unable or unwilling to provide for them. The Hospital for Invalid Gentlewomen was established almost immediately in Chandos Street, London in 1853. Florence Nightingale, Victorian woman par excellence, became superintendent of the hospital; it was her first administrative post. Miss Nightingale moved the institution to Harley Street, which had become the site of another project of the Governesses' Benevolent Association and, in the long term, a more important contribution. This "project" became Queen's College.

Intending not only to improve the lot of elderly and retired governesses without financial means, the committee planned to include courses of instruction for the future educators. Women who would become governesses need to be trained. "The vocation of a teacher is an awful one," is a phrase particularly characteristic of Maurice. The mere art of teaching is worthy of diligent study. Maurice believed, however, that the main qualification of a teacher was not merely an acquaintance with method, but a real grounded knowledge of that which is to be taught, and a sympathy with those who are to learn. Not every woman would necessarily become a governess, however, and Maurice proposed that the college which was projected by the association embrace all who would come: "How dared we deny that every lady is and must be a teacher — of some person or other, of children, sisters, the poor."[25] Maurice had for some time been actively engaged in teaching young men at King's College in the Strand, and had long been determined to include among his students the sisters of the boys he taught. Now was his opportunity.

Queen's College in Harley Street opened its doors in 1848. Maurice outlined the course of studies for the young women in his public lecture, *Queen's College, London, its Objects and Methods.* "Why are there no colleges for one sex as well as the other?" he asks. He proposed studies for women in no way different from the ideal curriculum which he proposed for young men. Drawing and music, of course, but also mathematics, natural philosophy, grammar, Latin, English literature, pedagogy, practical mechanics, geography, history, and finally and most important, theology. "It cannot be supposed that I change my tone and habit of speaking when I go from Harley Street to the Strand." Maurice felt a moral obligation, he declared, to "that sex whose influence must tell most powerfully upon ours." Needless to say, this work for women's education was not only questioned, but heartily attacked. Maurice was becoming more and more suspect because of his supposed political as well as religious views. It became necessary to defend the foundation of the college in a letter to the bishop of London; he invited the prelate to be the Visitor of the College and share his concern for the cause of women. There must come a time, Maurice writes, when "all the daughters of this land, of whatever order and degree, shall feel that they have a place in its spiritual history."[26]

The year of revolution also saw the coming together around their "prophet" of the group of young men who founded the cooperative movement and the community of thought called Christian Socialism. Enough has been said about the tragic and disgraceful events which, in 1854, led to Maurice's surrender of his professorship at King's College in the Strand. Whether his difficulties were due to the supposed heterodoxy of *Theological Essays,* published in 1854, or from the fear among conservatives of what was supposed to be his radical political and economic views, freedom from academic responsibility made possible the organization in 1854 of the Working Men's College, a people's college founded by the Christian Socialist movement. Eager to carry out some similar work for women, Maurice delivered a series of lectures, *Plan of a Female College for the Help of the Rich and the Poor.* Maurice proposed in these lectures to prepare women for careers as teachers as well as nurses. Women, he thought, were ideally suited to be teachers, although Maurice also asserts, "It seems to me that all men and women should feel themselves born to be teachers.... They must be communicating wisdom to others, or losing it themselves."[27] On May 21, 1855, classes began for working women.

These lectures were delivered in an atmosphere of suspicion, and there was much distrust of Maurice's motives. Never one to back down from anything he believed to be a fight against evil, Maurice defended this Working Women's College by attempting to draw the sting from his opponents. A woman's college was in no way a novelty, he declared; there were already female colleges in Harley Street, Bedford Square, and Hyde Park. "This college is to fit women for engaging in certain tasks which no other persons can perform equally well, as can be so helpful in teaching their countrymen to perform." There is a famous passage in the lecture which some have used to question Maurice's loyalty to the cause of women, but it is important to remember the time, and, in 1855, the tenuous position of the founder as well as of the embryo institution.

> I have guarded myself against the suspicion that I would educate ladies for the kind of tasks which belong to our professions....I not only do not see my way to such a result. I should not wish my college to lead to it. The best way to avoid it is to found such a college.[28]

In defense of Maurice's apparently sexist statement, it is important to remember that until the last half of our present century, the tradition still obtained whereby men did the major physical, commercial, and professional work in the world. Women reared children or worked in adjunctive helping and nursing professions. Whatever his intentions, Maurice's colleges for women played an important role in the history of women's rights. It is interesting that Lady Stanley, in her masterful record of the growth of women's higher education in England, traced a direct and clear line of development from Queen's College, Harley Street to the opening of the Medical College for Women in 1874, two years after Maurice's death.[29]

§5

The decade of the eighteen-sixties witnessed a dramatic development in the agitation for women's rights in England, and Maurice strongly supported each new cause. He was guided in this, as in everything, by his confidence in an underlying order which, although invisible, needed to be acknowledged and obeyed. A theological "digger," he sought not to build systems and edifices, but to go beneath outward appearances to a reality both true and everlasting. Loyal to Trinitarian principles, Maurice saw that the relationship between persons within the being of God was reflected directly in the idea of man-as-Image; women, he knew, were an integral part of that reflection and part of a unified whole.

Three particular issues allow us to examine the quality of Maurice's support. Beginning in 1864, legislation was introduced in Parliament which would guarantee the rights of married women to own property. Another focal point of political confrontation throughout these years of Maurice's life, the cause of women's suffrage, was a major concern in Britain. Finally, and involving a more subtle acknowledgment of the integrity of woman-as-Image, there was bitter conflict over first the passage, and then the repeal, of the Contagious Diseases Acts.

The question of married women's right to own property came up naturally as a part of Maurice's investigation of the relationship between the sexes in marriage, and he spoke to the issue in his series of lectures on *Social Morality* delivered at Cambridge University. Any relationship between persons was marked, he asserts, by a particular underlying "ethos," or character. The ethos of marriage is trust. The trust which is implied in the relation of husband and wife, he maintains, "would be wrongly appealed to by those who oppose any measures for protecting the distinct property of women. . . . Where the true ethos prevails, any rules about property will be unnecessary; the cry for rules is an intimation that it does not prevail."[30]

Upon the general admission of householders to the franchise in England, general legislation, introduced by John Stuart Mill, was proposed which would admit women of property to vote. Maurice saw that it was only a halfway measure, a way of stepping aside from the straight path for the sake of mere expedience. He supports the legislation, however, in a letter which appeared in the *Spectator* in March 1870. The achievement of the vote for women, he says there, is not important simply because it removes a constitutional anomaly — an anomaly created by the admission of householders to the franchise. Maurice claims, rather, that women's suffrage would be a positive strengthening of the *moral* life of England. It might be true, as many had said in opposition to women's suffrage, that women already possessed great domestic power, were indeed perhaps the most powerful force in the country. Nevertheless the right to vote, Maurice insists, would work to insure that the power women already possess "may be used seriously, with a deliberate conviction, with a dread of sacrificing general interests to private partialities." He argues that such power must be linked to a sense of responsibility, and viewed as a trust; this sense would be furthered by the extension of the franchise. For

> in any sphere where women feel their responsibility, they are, as a rule, far more conscientious than men. . . . When in any sphere they are less conscientious and help to make men less conscientious, it is a reasonable conjecture that in this sphere something has taken from them the sense of responsibility.[31]

Maurice's championship of the cause of women's suffrage was valued so highly that it was reprinted long after his lifetime, in the early years of our own century when the campaign for women's right to vote was nearing its ultimate victory.

In 1864, 1866, and 1869 acts of Parliament were passed which gave legal sanction to vice by placing prostitutes under police supervision, while also exposing them to cruel injustice. These Contagious Diseases Acts were applied first to seaports and garrison towns, but an attempt was also made to extend their enforcement to the entire country. By 1869, agitation against the Acts had grown to the extent that a Ladies' National Association for Repeal was formed, of which Josephine Butler was secretary. Support was quick in coming from such influential Englishwomen as Florence Nightingale, Harriet Martineau, and Lydia Becker. Mrs. Butler, indefatigable in her efforts toward repeal, opposed and defeated several Parliamentary candidates who supported the acts in the by-elections of 1870 and 1872. In March 1871 she gave evidence before a royal commission which had been appointed in deference to the agitation, and of which Maurice was a member.

Maurice's own involvement in the affair is a good example of social concern for the welfare of women and, equally, demonstrates how he was able to weigh contrary points of view and eventually change his own position in a controversy. In January 1870 he wrote his son Edmund that he had signed a petition in favor of the act,

> being grieved by the plight of the innocent persons who suffered for the guilty and by the general [belief] that all kinds of disease should be dealt with, as well as they can be, medically. . . . But I suspect that I did not take enough into consideration the injury which might be done to the woman by recognizing, in any degree, her degradation as part of a System. That recognition seems to be shocking and if I have any degree assisted to it, I am bound to consider earnestly what I can do for the object which Mrs. Butler has at heart.[32]

Maurice eventually voted with Josephine Butler in opposition to Parliamentary legislation dealing with prostitution. It was characteristic of his attitude, however, that Maurice's attempts to combat prostitution were in accord with his whole attitude toward human society and the sexes.

He espoused positive action when necessary, but thought it was far more important to help young women as well as young men to discover who they were: both singly, and together, created in the image of God. "If the tone of young men's thoughts about women could be raised — if the thoughts of the young women about themselves and their relations with men can be raised, the effect will come more completely, even more rapidly, than if a vain effort was made to put prostitution down."[33] As always, Maurice placed his hope in education, in the bringing to light of the inner nature of man-as-Image of God, in leading society to discover the truth of an order which lay at its foundation, an order seen best in the relationships between human beings which reflect the Trinitarian nature of the being of God. Together as male and female, men and women must discover that they are created in God's image. The relationship of the sexes for Maurice is meant to be symbiotic, a relationship of mutual interdependence in which each person fills a very basic need for the other. Such a relationship echoes a primordial, cosmic unity in the being of God. As the reflection of the divine nature, before any separation or distinction, there is a wholeness and unity in which opposites are contained.

But within any discussion of the sexes it is important to realize that there are differences, opposites, tensions between them which result in creativity. An analysis of any moment of creation, in the mind either of a single individual or of a vigorous society, reveals what is described as contrasexual forces coming together in such a way as to bring about something new and different. These opposite forces stand in dynamic tension within any particular human being, as within any community. Such contrasexual forces in creative tension can be illustrated, for example, in the way that Maurice consistently worked with undergraduates. His son and biographer records that in the final years of his life, Maurice, then

Knightbridge Professor at the University, was surrounded by his students at Cambridge. In small groups it was his custom always to "get some young lady who would break the ice. . . . He had a succession of young lady visitors who so helped him." Afterward, he would go to his wife and say, "Fancy this child drawing out all these young men."[34]

There is a significance in this little drama which took place over and over again in Saint Peter's Terrace, Maurice's house in Cambridge. For him, here was the feminine at its best. Free herself, a woman is able to draw out the male because of her own confidence in who she is, and make it possible for him to become what he was meant to be. Woman, Maurice continually asserts, is to be the instructor and the counselor of the man. She can only succeed in such a calling if she is indeed herself and can acknowledge her position as an equal part, the complementary half of that whole in which the being of God is reflected.

Maurice has often been called the apostle of unity, of wholeness. He thought that one of the most important contributions of the feminine is to bring men as well as women to an awareness of this wholeness, the unity of the human race. Women make it possible for men to think of themselves not as members of a little body, but as part of "the great family to which they belong by birthright."[35] All too often, Maurice observes, because of the tendency of education, a man trained in a specialty or profession might easily come to consider himself less a man than a lawyer, a soldier, or a clergyman. It is one of the distinctive functions of women to be ministers and witnesses of wholeness, of that unity which reflects the community of equals.

[55]

Maurice's insight into this aspect of the feminine vocation is in line with the view that the human psyche contains the power to look at things and to analyze them into their component parts. This power of intellect, sometimes spoken of as masculine focused awareness, gives us the ability to formulate ideas and the capacity to change, invent, and create. Also within the human psyche there is what may be called *diffused* awareness, in which everything is linked with everything else. This is an attitude of receptivity, of acceptance, a consciousness of the unity of all life and a readiness for relationship. We must realize that both of these qualities are intrinsically present in the nature of every human being to a greater or lesser degree, but it may still be possible to speak of a masculine *focused* awareness, and of a feminine *diffused* awareness, an awareness of relationship and unity.

The meaning of Communion was not a matter of the intellect for Maurice, but of another faculty which would reveal the nature of the relationship of each member of the human family to the whole and to the Triune God that lay at the foundation and heart of all. He claimed

> the existence of a faculty capable of distinguishing between spiritual truth and falsehood, between right and wrong, which he believed to be universal among men, however obscured it may often have become; his belief that this faculty is independent of the intellect, often made him refer back in thoughts to the sick beds of Guy's Hospital. . . .36

Maurice attributes the gift of understanding the Communion as showing forth the unity of the human family, redeemed in Christ as head of the race, to that spiritual faculty apart from intellect. It is a matter of diffused awareness, the feminine power for comprehending relationships.

This idea of the feminine vocation helps us to see the import of Maurice's last words, carefully recorded by the little crowd of men and women who gathered around his bedside. Maurice had just received Communion, and it seemed to absorb all his thoughts. The Communion, he said with his last breath, is for all nations and peoples, and "something too, we understood, about it being *women's work* to teach men its meaning."[37]

MAURICE

ON

PRAYER

"The best way to understand a theologian is not to analyze the fine points of his clever controversial works,
but rather to enter into the heart of his spiritual meditations, those works in which the theologian is cultivating
fellowship with God and most forgetting himself."

JOHN ORENS

There is no Anglican theologian of the nineteenth century more universally revered than Frederick Denison Maurice. Christian Socialist, educator, ecumenist, novelist, and priest, Maurice looms above most of his contempories in the breadth of his interests and the prophetic spirit which inspired them. Identified with no church party, yet claimed by all, Maurice seems the quintessential Anglican: learned, tolerant, and pious. But as soon as one begins to study Maurice, paradoxes rise at every turn. In his own day, far from seeing in him a prophet or the embodiment of the *via media*, many writers complained that he was incomprehensibility incarnate — if not an outright heretic. "That Maurice is a man of great powers as well as of great earnestness, is proved," lamented John Henry Newman, "but for myself I ever thought him hazy, and thus lost interest in his writings." Leslie Stephen was less charitable. "Of all the muddle-headed, intricate, futile persons I have ever studied," he complained, "[Maurice] was about the most utterly bewildering."[1]

This perplexity was not confined to the nineteenth century,

for in our own century scholars have had little difficulty demonstrating the contradictions in his politics, and the Platonic conundrums in his theology. Most recently, Stephen Sykes has charged Maurice with "intellectual laziness and self-deception," and argues that much of our current theological malaise can be laid at Maurice's doorstep. As if to add insult to injury, the *Incomplete Book of Failures*, the official handbook of the Not-Terribly-Good Club of Great Britain, lists Maurice as the world's worst preacher, citing Aubrey de Vere's observation: "Listening to him was like eating pea soup with a fork."[2]

Yet frustratingly obscure though they have often found him, Anglicans have never failed to be struck by the saintliness of Maurice's character. When he was chaplain of Lincoln's Inn, people flocked to services because of his reverent conduct of the daily office. Ordinary men and women, who could no more understand him than could Aubrey de Vere, remarked that there was an unusual power in his prayers. Indeed, many people "said that for the first time they understood the force of a prayer after hearing him." Those who knew Maurice well regarded him with something akin to awe. "There is about that man," remarked a Cambridge acquaintance, *"theion ti pathos* [a divine pain]." Five university men, pondering whom they would trust to accompany them during their last hours on earth, agreed that each of them "should write down the name of the person he would choose; and the papers when opened were found to contain a single name — Maurice." Faced with the contradiction between this universally acknowledged sanctity and the almost equally universal complaints about his obscurity and even heterodoxy, more than a few observers have thrown up their hands in dismay. "That so good a man should be mistaken," confessed Canon Liddon, "is a very perplexing mystery of the moral world. . . ."[3]

But perplexed though Liddon and many others have been, we need not be. Maurice himself has provided the solution to the puzzle of holiness and seeming hazy-mindedness. The best way to understand a theologian, he once wrote, is not to analyze the fine points of his clever controversial works, but rather to enter into the heart of his spiritual meditations, those works in which the theologian is cultivating fellowship with God and most forgetting himself. This may seem unexceptional enough, but in Maurice's case it leads to a remarkable conclusion. The principal criticism directed against Maurice is that he is obscure. Maurice, it is charged, waffles on almost every issue, uses words in the loosest possible way, embraces contradictory positions, and then announces that this unholy amalgam is the *via media*. These accusations are plausible enough; Maurice does try to see problems from every conceivable point of view. He does strain the meaning of words. And he does try to draw together ideas which most people regard as mutually exclusive. Maurice does not do so because he is confused. He does so because he is a visionary whose theology is a fervent defense of the primacy of prayer over argument, and of communion with God over what he likes to dismiss as "mere notions."[4] Our task, then, is not to glean from Maurice's writings helpful maxims on prayer, although we will certainly find some. Rather, it is to reveal the heart of Maurice's theology — the union of God and humanity in Christ — which is the foundation and the goal of prayer.

Maurice lived in an age very much like our own, an age characterized by social unrest and religious doubt. Those not set on overturning society seemed concerned with nothing but the pursuit of wealth. "Our age," sighed Dr. Pusey, "is in general too busy, too active, for deep aspirations after God. . . ." To be sure, the Church had no lack of zealous supporters. But instead of addressing the needs of the new industrial society growing up around them, Anglicans were at each other's throats, locked in fierce combat to determine whether the Establishment was to be Catholic, Evangelical, or liberal. How then could people pray? "The great body of Englishmen is becoming utterly indifferent to us all," Maurice observed gloomily in 1850, "smile grimly and contemptuously at our controversies and believe that no help is to come to their suffering from any of us."[5] To many Victorians God had become a remote abstraction, a possibility to be clung to rather than a redeemer in whom they could trust. Wrote Tennyson:

> Behold we know not anything;
> I can but trust that good shall fall
> At last — far off — at last, to all,
> And every winter change to spring.
>
> So runs my dream; but what am I?
> An infant crying in the night;
> An infant crying for the light,
> And with no language but a cry.
> "In Memoriam"

With God so remote, from whence could come spiritual solace? One bold answer was to locate the attributes of God in our own hearts. Salvation would then be close at hand because we would be the very font of divinity. Theology, the German philosopher Ludwig Feuerbach trumpeted, must be replaced by anthropology.[6] Maurice was painfully aware of the religious anguish of his generation, and understood better than most Christians the desire to be done with an unapproachable deity. But his answer to the longing of his age is radically different from that of philosophers like Feuerbach. It is not theology which should be replaced by anthropology, but anthropology which must be transformed into theology. We cannot save the world by looking to ourselves. Rather, our hope lies in the fact that we live, move, and have our being in Jesus Christ. Far from being cut off from God, we are partakers of the divine nature. To those who would see prayer as the desperate cry of lost souls to the vast unknown, Maurice proclaims that prayer is the most truly human activity. Indeed, it is only in prayer, only as we experience communion with God, that we can see the world as it truly is.[7] To those who lived in darkness, Maurice brought the light of the Incarnation.

Unfortunately, Maurice complains, theologians seem intent upon obscuring this message of hope. They are full of clever proofs for the existence of a Supreme Being. Of opinions about the nature of the Godhead there is no end. But what the world needs, Maurice insists, is a Father to save it, a Father to give men and women the power to do the good they long to do.[8] Rather than being an occasion for philosophical debates, the Christian proclamation of the fatherhood of God is proof against abstractions and a deliverance from what Maurice calls "the uncertainties of opinion." Moreover, by treating God as a metaphysical entity, however holy and awesome, theologians have severed the bond between God and our race established in Christ. Not only does this make it impossible to understand God, it makes it impossible for us to understand ourselves. With the same fervor with which he exalts the fatherhood of God, Maurice also preaches the sonship of humanity. This, indeed, is the Gospel: "the revelation or unveiling of a mystery hidden from ages and generations," the mystery of "the true constitution of humanity in Christ." Not to claim for ourselves this union with Christ, in fact, is "to believe and to act a lie." It is also to make prayer all but impossible, for there could be no true worship except when we see our "own nature glorified at God's right hand."[9]

The fact that countless numbers of men and women, living in an ostensibly Christian nation, did not claim the privileges of sons and daughters of God was a scandal for which Maurice blamed the infidelity of the Church. Lip service might be given to the fatherhood of God, he charges, but both Roman and Protestant divines have made the Fall "the foundation of Theology," reducing the incarnation and death of Christ to mere "provisions against the effects of it." Ministers of every denomination were thundering all sorts of gospels from their pulpits save that gospel proclaimed by Saint Paul: that the mystery of Christ is the ground of all things in heaven and earth. But this was only the beginning of the problem. In severing divinity from humanity, the religious world had severed the life of the Church from the life of the family.[10]

This is a matter of far greater importance than it may first appear. God, Maurice notes, did not create individuals; rather, "male and female he created them." We are members of a kind, of a society, of which the family is the fundamental unit. The family, therefore, is no accident of history; God has established it because God himself is social. Just as each of us is made in the image of God, so the life of every family is intended to be a mirror of the divine life of mutual sacrifice. "The earthly image and the heavenly archetype will always sustain and illustrate one another," explains Maurice. "The family on earth will be best when it confesses the family in heaven. The family in heaven will always be drawing into itself, always investing with its light and glory, the families on earth."[11] This being the case, to treat the family as a purely earthly institution, to treat the social bonds between human beings as if they were of no account, is to undermine faith in God and to pervert the purpose of prayer. Worship of the divine community, Maurice is convinced, can only be offered effectively by men and women conscious of their membership in the redeemed human community.

It is utter madness, therefore, to try to frighten people into praying. Maurice knows as well as anyone that when the human spirit exalts itself, when it attempts to live apart from God, it sinks into slavery and sin. But he also understands that before surrender to God can be commended as the way of life, men and women must first be assured of God's love and freed from the self-loathing which they confuse with Christian humility. God has not cast us off so that we must seek him, Maurice told his parishioners; it is we who have cast God off, yet he continues to bring us into union with himself. The Church's invitation to prayer, therefore, is not the command to grovel before an omnipotent tyrant in the hope of currying his favor. Whatever its ministers might say, the voice of the Church is beckoning and full of comfort: "Come, because God is with you now — because intercourse with Him now is essential to your life here as well as hereafter — because without it you cannot do the works of men, and possess the rights of men." It is when we hear this voice that we shall be able to cry out at last: "Source of all life and goodness, where art Thou? It is thyself and not any of thy treasures that I need. Take them away if Thou wilt not reveal thyself while I possess them. Take them away if they hinder me from the revelation of thyself."[12]

But dare I, sinner that I am, expect an answer to my plea? To this, one of the most disturbing questions that can be raised about prayer, Maurice replies by turning again to the Incarnation. "If Christ were not at [God's] right hand," he confesses, "I might think, 'Some of us may pray to Him, some that are good,' but may I pray to Him who feel I am not good? Believing that He who died and went unto the grave and into hell for us all is at the right hand of the Father Almighty forever," Maurice concludes confidently, "I believe that we may all cry to Him and that He will hear us all and own us all as members of his family."[13]

Again and again Maurice returns to the universal reconciliation between God and the human race which has been wrought by Christ and which makes prayer possible. Christ did not die and rise again, he declares, "to give a few proud Philosophers or . . . ascetical Pharisees some high notions about the powers of the soul and the meanness of the body." No, Christ "entered into the state of the lowest beggar, of the poorest, stupidest, wickedest wretch whom that Philosopher or that Pharisee can trample upon," in order that he might "redeem the humanity which Philosophers, Pharisees, beggars, and harlots share together." It is because this is so that Maurice can assure the doubtful that "there can be no act so entirely suitable to man, so thoroughly joyful, as that of thanking and blessing God."[14]

At first glance, only Maurice's tone — his patience with sceptics, his solicitude for the poor and the outcast — may seem remarkable. But Maurice's understanding of the reconciliation of God and humanity, and of its implications for our spiritual lives, startled and scandalized his contemporaries. For these, there was no disputing the fact that Christ Jesus came into the world to save sinners. But whom had Jesus reconciled with the Father? The converted, answered Evangelicals and Protestant Dissenters. The baptized, answered Tractarians and Roman Catholics. Everyone, answered Maurice.

Baptism, he readily admits, is the sign of admission into the kingdom of God. This wonderful sacrament, Maurice writes, "gives the spirit and power whence repentance and every right act must flow; it brings the subject of it under the discipline of that purifying force whereby the old and evil nature is to be consumed."[15] But baptism does not make us sons and daughters of God, because Christ has already done so on the Cross. Far from severing our ties with the unredeemed mass of mankind, baptism gives us the right to claim an inheritance won for humanity as a whole. The particularity of the Church, he argues, reveals the universal destiny of the race.

The most obvious consequence of Maurice's extraordinary understanding of redemption is that those condemned by the religious world as standing outside the realm of God's grace are, in fact, bound up with us in Christ and subject to the same Spirit as are we. Thus instead of denigrating the spiritual aspirations of the unchurched, Christians have a responsibility to show tender solicitude toward these promptings of the Spirit, and to teach the world that inspiration "is the proper law and order of the world." No one, insists Maurice, "ought to write, or speak, or think, except under the acknowledgment of an inspiration...." The great sin of the rationalist poets of the eighteenth century, he observes wisely, was not that they invoked the Muse, but that they did not believe in its existence. This does not mean that Christians should adopt an attitude of indiscriminate reverence for every creation of the human mind. What Maurice does enjoin is humility and the chastened recognition that we can pray only as "representatives of restored humanity."[16]

Maurice's theology of redemptive union with Christ can open our eyes to the presence of the Spirit both in our own lives and in the lives of those who seem much farther from Christ. His insistence on this bond between humanity and God also offers a solution to the difficult and often painful problem of sin and repentance. No one could be more outspoken than Maurice about the gravity of our baptismal vows and of our inability to hold fast to them. The possibility that earnest men and women, faced with the awful certainty of sin, would turn aside from the Christian life in despair was ever before him. It was as a remedy for this difficulty that Pusey and the other Tractarians had urged the revival of auricular confession. The sinner, having received the counsel and absolution of a priest, could go forth from the confessional knowing that his relationship with God had been reestablished. But what the Oxford Apostolicals offered as balm for the soul, Maurice regards with suspicion as a likely hindrance to Christian faith and prayer. Indeed, it was Pusey's treatment of post-baptismal sin which led Maurice to turn against the Oxford Movement. "I remember to this day the misery [Pusey's tract] caused me," he wrote to his son many years later. "I saw that I must be hopelessly and forever estranged from this doctrine...unless I abandoned all my hopes for myself and for the world."[17]

Maurice had no objection to those troubled in conscience seeking out a priest for absolution. The Book of Common Prayer commended the practice, and shrill denunciations would not stop worried penitents from making their confessions. In part, Maurice's concern is that the more conscious such penitents become of their own sins, the more they will fall into that self-centeredness which is the root of sin. Maurice fears, moreover, that frequent resort to priestly absolution will lead to the dangerous belief that the power to absolve is a clerical possession rather than a gift from God. But what most troubled Maurice was his conviction that the Tractarians were raising doubts about the cornerstone of the Christian life: the bond between God and humanity in Christ. In baptism, Maurice insists, we do not acquire a new nature; nothing is infused into us. Rather, we are incorporated into Christ. To claim, as Pusey had, that the baptismal purity lost in sin could never be restored, is to treat our bond with Christ as a mere object which it is our duty to keep spotless. Prayer under these circumstances could become an almost intolerable burden.[18]

The fact that neither conversion nor confession are necessary to reestablish our bond with God does not mean that the two are unimportant. All of us need to recognize afresh the grace of God, and to cease resisting the Spirit which is already at work in our lives. But instead of restoring us to God's favor, our penitence simply enables us to exclaim joyfully: "I was asleep, now I am awake." As for the priest who is hearing confessions, Maurice cautions against probing too deeply into the particular sins of those who seek his counsel. Above all, the priest is to avoid setting penances which give the impression that God must be compensated in some way. Let the priest simply explain that God has sent him to declare the forgiveness of sins for Christ's sake, and bid the penitent receive forgiveness and accept reconciliation.[19]

§2

Reconciled, forgiven, bound up in Christ, we stand at the gates of heaven. Indeed, it is in the very act of acknowledging our dependence on our loving Father that we embark on the adventure of Christian prayer, the essence of which is the surrender of self-will for God's will. Just as in baptism we are not led to seek a new nature of our own, but to accept our incorporation into Christ, so in our prayers we are not "to work ourselves into a right state," or to "raise ourselves to some individual excellence," but simply to set our minds on God, yielding ourselves "to the Spirit who dwells in the whole body."[20]

Maurice does not mean by this that we are to embrace a slave-like docility, for he knows well that men and women cannot surrender themselves unless they have already grown into selfhood. Moreover, to crush our own faculties and so to seek self-annihilation is itself a reckless act of self-indulgence and an insult to God, who has given us our talents. Jesus, Maurice points out, came not to be an example of self-sacrifice, but to serve and glorify God. It is this particular kind of self-denial which is the ground of our existence, because it was the ground of Christ's. "There is to be no struggle after saintship," Maurice writes, "no wild efforts after perfection. It is God's will to sanctify us; we come to ask that He will do that will for us and in us." Above all, we need not affect that sham tranquility which masquerades as Christian piety. "Shall we tell men how they may regulate themselves so that they may present a comely face to the world, distracted by no tumults, perplexed by no doubts?" Maurice asks angrily.

Or shall we speak to them as the Church herself speaks to them, declaring that God verily manifested Himself, not to the eye, but to the spirit, and that His Spirit is working with their spirits that they may be clean and pure within?[21]

To yield ourselves to God in prayer, of course, requires a surrender of those selfish objects which are often at the heart of our petitions. Every devout Christian, Maurice observes, "learns soon that passionate eagerness to get some good for himself," even if it be the salvation of his soul, "is the greatest possible hindrance to prayer." For one thing, "we are likely to mistake grievously what we want; to charge God foolishly for not giving us that which could profit us; at last, to dream that we have found a treasure which puffs us up with vanity and proves worthless." Instead of finding God, we are plunged back into the narrow and stifling world of sin and death. To be sure, such misguided prayer is easy, but this only makes it all the more dangerous: "The selfish object which we seek," warns Maurice with an insight born of experience,

floats before our minds — if it be an earthly object, palpably; if an invisible object, in happy images, having more in them of terror than of beauty — but the object, he to whom our prayer is addressed, is afar off, of him there is scarcely the least discernment.[22]

Not only do selfish prayers cut us off from God, they cut us off from the rest of humanity. We are no more redeemed alone and in isolation from others, Maurice insists, than we are created alone. It is humanity itself, he writes, which "has been purified and regenerated by its union with the Godhead." Thus we can rightly pray only as members of the human family, and it is for that family that Christ bids us intercede.[23]

[73]

This is the root of Maurice's Christian Socialism. It is easy to point out that Maurice abhorred the radical changes which true socialism demands, but criticisms of his political timidity are hopelessly beside the point. Maurice was not a reformer but a prophet, and what concerns him is the fact that our life with God is inextricably bound up in our relations with our neighbors. Faith in God, he writes, is the ground of human citizenship, but that citizenship in turn makes us fit for communion with God. So intimate is the connection between the two, Maurice argues, that the principal reason why people do not trust God is that they themselves are guilty of defrauding their neighbors. On the importance of this point for both prayer and the future of the Church, Maurice is clear and insistent. The individualistic religion of his own time, he cries out, is in danger of reducing church services to "foul orgies of Mammon worship." And Maurice warns that the establishment of a "middle class religion" would oppress the people as they had never been oppressed before. Denied the gospel, the masses would turn to atheism.[24]

Were that surrender of the self which Maurice advocates so passionately a work which we had to do on our own, it is difficult to see how anyone could pray or even attempt to pray. But Maurice insists in a thoroughly orthodox fashion that it is the Spirit, through the grace of Christ, which prays in us. Indeed, few nineteenth-century theologians emphasized the role of the Spirit more than did Maurice. Christians, he contends,

> never will understand Apostles and Prophets, they never will reverence Apostles and Prophets, they never will believe Apostles and Prophets, till they confess that the Holy Ghost who spoke by them has not forsaken us, that we are baptized into His

Name, that we are able to perceive anything, hope for anything, love anything, only because He walks with us and in us.[25]

It would be easy to conclude from this that rather than making prayer an arduous discipline, Maurice teaches that all we need do is wait for some remarkable divine intervention to make us pray. But Maurice is quick to warn of the perils of just such an attitude.

To regard the operation of the Holy Spirit as a series of dramatic interruptions of the natural course of events, he points out, is not a sign of faith at all; rather, it is the obverse side of materialism. The Methodist revival was a perfect case in point: "It seemed so utterly strange to men in the eighteenth century, that human beings should exhibit any spiritual feelings or energies," Maurice observes, "that the appearance of them was almost necessarily looked upon as something not wonderful merely, but startling; not the effect of a divine influence merely, but of a magical one." The truth, writes Maurice, is "that every operation in nature, the growth of every tree, the budding of every flower, should be referred to the influence of him who first moved upon the face of the waters." If this were true of nature, how much truer is it of the human soul. Maurice is convinced that we must attribute "every act of our minds, every exercise of our affections, every energy of our will, to [the Holy] Spirit." Even when our minds are wrongly directed, they are rightly inspired. Were this not so, prayer could be little more than soothsaying.[26]

Thus Christians are not to wait upon the Spirit before praying, as the Quakers do, nor are they to look fearfully for signs of the Spirit's presence in order to convince themselves that they have indeed surrendered themselves. Just as the distinctive mark of the

New Testament minister was his placing himself under the habitual guidance of the Spirit poured out after Christ's glorification, so regular prayer, in season and out, is one of the distinctive characteristics of Christian spirituality. It is worth emphasizing that Maurice did not merely share the Anglican suspicion that "violent impulses may produce prayers that are selfish, and little better than curses." What is at stake for him is the character of God. Christians do not worship angels who come down and trouble the waters from time to time, he remarks sharply, for their faith is in an eternal Spirit who is always moving on the face of the deep. For much the same reason, when Christians do pray they are not to expect what commonly passes for the miraculous. Bound as we are to Christ, inspired by the Holy Spirit, we no longer need evidence that we are children of God rather than victims of natural forces. Miracles may still take place, Maurice readily admits. But most of the miracles being hawked about are either lies or wonders of no religious value, for they turn our mind away from God.[27]

Included in this indictment of miracle-seeking is the seemingly selfless desire for extraordinary spiritual gifts, such as that of speaking in tongues, a prize as highly regarded by some Christians in the Victorian era as it is today. Unlike many of his contemporaries, Maurice did not ridicule those who practiced glossolalia. Rather, he argues that these enthusiasts have mistaken the spectacular events of Pentecost for the abiding miracle they signify: the common fellowship of Gentile and Jew in Christ, and the continual indwelling of the Holy Spirit in the heart of every believer. The argument sometimes advanced, that the miraculous ability to speak an obscure language would be a boon to missionaries, Maurice regards as further evidence of the dangers of what we would call

Pentecostalism. The last thing a messenger of the gospel needs is a supernatural power that would only puff up his pride; the gift he does need, claims Maurice, is one already vouchsafed. It is an "actual living sympathy with the creatures whom he addresses," a recognition that he shares their human nature.[28] In the things of the Spirit, as in all of life, the beginning of wisdom is to recognize our common destiny as sons and daughters of God.

We know that we must pray and, Maurice has assured us, we know that by the grace of God we can pray. But *how* are we to pray? How can we bring the breadth and universality of the temple into the closet?[29] Maurice is as suspicious of notions about prayer as he is of notions about God. But he does point to the Lord's Prayer as a model for our imitation, for here, he writes, private prayer becomes common prayer. We pray not only for ourselves, but for our family and our race as well. Maurice is aware of the danger that the Lord's Prayer might become a charm rather than an example, and that its frequent use may rob it of meaning, so he suggests that it be prayed clause by clause, with ample time allowed for meditation on the meaning of all too familiar words. Thus the power of each clause and each petition can be realized in its full significance.

We begin then, as our Savior Christ has taught us, "Our Father who art in heaven." Pause here, says Maurice, and ponder what it means to say that God is our Father. This is no metaphysical puzzle, but the declaration that we are loved, that our family ties are sacred, as are our duties to one another as children of one Father. Thus when we pray, "Hallowed be thy name," we renounce superstition, we renounce the gloomy and tyrannical God of popular Protestantism, and we renounce whatever theological views we possess which could narrow the sphere of God's grace. To hallow the name of God — Father, Son, and Holy Spirit — is to do what God would have us do: to be just to our own children, and to love our neighbors as ourselves.[30]

This is not simply a matter of personal relations, sacred though they may be. Christ bids us pray, "Thy kingdom come, thy will be done, on earth as it is in heaven." We know that God reigns and that we are citizens of a heavenly kingdom. Yet all around us, in the very world which God has redeemed, are the evidences of human wickedness. In praying for the coming of God's kingdom, then, we commit ourselves to the cause of the poor and the oppressed. "O arise!" Maurice would have us cry. "Let us not have the upper hand." Even when we pray for something as simple as our daily bread, our thoughts should always be with others. To be sure, we are not to forget ourselves altogether. But we must ever keep in mind the horrible fact that while a few of us have more than we can consume, many more are starving. As long as such injustice festers, Maurice warns, revolutions must come. This is as much a challenge to the complacency of liberals as it is to the indifference of conservatives. "You clever men," Maurice writes mockingly, "you great liberals, have found out that there are no evil spirits who hold the bodies and spirits of men bound in fearful misery and captivity. Every street and alley in every city of Europe laughs your wisdom to scorn."[31]

It is little wonder that we next pray, "Forgive us our trespasses, as we forgive those who trespass against us." Maurice is quick to point out that forgiveness is not a private transaction in which the deity rewards us for good behavior. When we are forgiven, and when we forgive, we enter into that universal forgiveness which is God's alone. Thus we are asking that we may receive "a real and perpetual spring of forgiveness" within ourselves; a spring, in turn, which we can only receive when we forgive others. So too, when we ask that we may be spared temptation, we are not begging for personal willpower, but confessing God's sovereignty over the world. The circumstances of our lives are God's, not ours, and we pray that they will not prove to be the occasions for us to do evil. We must remember that God has triumphed over sin and death, and that we are bidden to enter into his triumph. This is by no means easy to do, Maurice warns, for the Christian life is one of perpetual conflicts: "You will have to battle not with flesh and blood only, but with principalities and powers, with the rulers and spiritual wickedness in high places." These demonic forces will try to persuade you that all is lost, that you cannot claim the blessing of God. But that blessing has already been won for you by Christ. You must claim it, Maurice says, "lest your life be a lie."[32]

The essence of this blessing is nothing other than communion with God. Not to experience it is the greatest tragedy which can befall a human being, for "we know that none of us can live, that we cannot live for one hour apart from Christ, the Son of God." For Maurice, as for all the great Christian spiritual writers, the goal of prayer and of life itself is that the soul becomes conscious of its intimate union with its Savior. "The highest, clearest, most spiritual idea of God which any creature can attain to," he writes,

is not that which he receives from a dream about the attributes of omnipresence, but that into which he enters when he contemplates the fulness of truth, and holiness, and love, the absolute perfect Being pleasing to identify himself with a human soul and body, to suffer with them, to raise them out of death, to raise them to glory.[33]

All our prayers and meditation lead us to the moment when we are ready to heed the voice which says: "Be still and know that I am God." Before we understood the high estate to which we are called, we would not have dared be still. Instead we would have cowered before the unknowable deity we hoped to appease, uttering long prayers, speaking in tongues, perhaps even torturing ourselves as Hindu holy men were said to do. But now we are sure that our loving Father is near us, and that we can indeed know him. The knowledge we seek, of course, does not consist of bits and pieces of information. To truly know God "is to find a centre to which we can refer ourselves and all things else; it is to find the ground upon which we are standing, to feel that which we did not create, which is and which must abide." It is in contemplative prayer such as this that we plumb "those amazing abysses which the reason seeks after, in which she delights, wonders and is lost."[34] This is the realm of the Name of God.

But even a personal experience as awesome as this, is but a way station in the life of the spirit. Convinced that the very heart of the gospel is the reconciliation which Christ has wrought between God and humanity, Maurice will not be content with a private vision, however sublime. Complete communion with Christ is vouchsafed to each of us and to the whole human family in the Eucharist. Indeed, he writes, the Eucharist "clears the mists from the nature of prayer, by bearing such a witness of the grace of our Lord Jesus Christ as prayer alone cannot bear." Those eager for a discussion of the intricacies of eucharistic theology itself will scour the works of Maurice in vain. Like Richard Hooker and many Anglicans since, Maurice regarded most of the controversies about the nature of Christ's presence at the altar as ill conceived and hopelessly beside the point. Christ, Maurice insists, "never has scorned, and never will scorn, any one who seeks not to defend this Sacrament, or to make theories about it, but to receive it." Indeed, the survival of Christianity as a living truth in the human heart, rather than as a mere collection of notions and generalizations, "depends mainly on the question of whether the Eucharist shall or shall not be acknowledged as the bond of universal life, and the means whereby men become partakers of it."[35]

What Maurice advocates is not the lazy tolerance of the spiritually indifferent; rather, he objects to spinning out notions about the Eucharist because they obscure the awful mystery of the sacrament. The institution of the Lord's Supper, he writes, was no passing ceremony, nor were Christ's words mere similes, as if Jesus were not the Son of Man and the Son of God. At that paschal meal, when the disciples ate the bread and drank the wine, they received "all the spiritual blessings which through the union of the Godhead with human flesh, the heirs of flesh might inherit...." For us, as for them, Christ is truly present. For us, as for them, there is communion with him and with all the saints. This mystery, Maurice believes, is too great to be contained within the eucharistic elements. To argue otherwise is to reduce Christ's presence to a meaningless merger of spirituality and locality into "vacant ubiquity." "Surely what we need," he writes, "is that [the elements] should be made a perfectly transparent medium through which this glory may be manifested, that nothing should be really beheld by the spirit of the worshippers but he into whose presence they are brought."[36]

[81]

What matters, then, is that in the Eucharist Christ has given us a bond between heaven and earth, "a witness that the Son of Man is set down at the right of the throne of God, and that those who believe in him, and suffer with him, are meant to live and reign with him there." There is in the Eucharist an assurance that with all our burdens and all our darkness we can come into the light of God. We find in this great sacrament, moreover, not only a bond between ourselves and our neighbors. Our intimacy with God at the altar, Maurice writes, should bring us closer to the parish family so that we may discover what can be done "in the best, simplest, most childlike way, for making others sharers in [our] blessings, physical, intellectual, and spiritual." For all of us, the Eucharist points beyond itself to that final consummation when the servants of the Lord "shall see His Face, and His Name shall be on their foreheads, and there shall be no night, and they shall need no candle, neither light of the Sun, for the Lord God will give them light, and they shall reign for ever and ever."[37]

Maurice was a man possessed by the vision of the world as it really is: redeemed, sanctified, and made anew. Like that of many visionaries, his prose is sometimes obscure and frequently longwinded. He belabors the obvious, he uses words in unconventional and even unjustifiable ways, and he sees his theology mirrored in almost everything he reads from the Scriptures to the Athanasian Creed. John Stuart Mill complained with some justification about Maurice's belief

> that the Church of England had known everything from the first, and that all the truths on the ground of which the Church and orthodoxy have been attacked (many of which he saw as clearly as any one) are not only consistent with the Thirty-Nine

[82]

Articles, but are better understood and expressed in those articles
than by any one who rejects them.[38]

Paradoxically, Maurice's greatest failing, particularly in his treatment of prayer, is that he falls into the very one-sidedness about
which he complains so passionately. Determined to challenge the
sentimental and selfish pietism of so much of Victorian religion,
Maurice advocated a spirituality which, on the face of it, left vir-
tually no room for individuals to pray for themselves. Appalled by
the popular view of prayer as a means of currying favor with God,
he was reluctant to give advice on techniques of prayer; indeed,
the very idea of spiritual direction distressed him. Moreover, in his
effort to convince men and women that they have already been redeemed, Maurice sometimes gives the mistaken impression that he
believes sin to be nothing more than ignorance, so that human beings can save themselves simply by recognizing what their true
state is.

Yet anyone who sets forth on the journey of prayer will find
in Maurice a wise and compassionate soul friend. Those paralyzed
by the haunting suspicion that God is a vengeful tyrant will learn
the joy of crying, "Abba! Father!" The overly scrupulous, weighed
down by sin and convinced that they can neither pray nor expect
their cries to be heard, will discover from Maurice that they are
children of God in whom the Spirit already moves and speaks. In-
tellectuals, convinced that they must build a Babel Tower of theology to scale the heavens, will find that God is ready to reach down
and touch them if they will but tear down the barrier erected by
their pride. To those who would yield to the temptation of retreat-
ing from the world to the realm of a purely private spirituality,
Maurice speaks unambiguously of the inseparability of prayer and

justice. And to those deluded by the ever-fashionable belief that spiritual freedom can only be achieved by abandoning the God of the Scriptures for some metaphysical abstraction, Maurice insists passionately that nothing less than a divine person can satisfy their longings, or free them from the tyranny of superstition.

"Orthodoxy," writes Kenneth Leech, "is about being consumed by glory: the word does not mean 'right belief' (as dictionaries tell us) but right *doxa*, right glory. To be orthodox is to be set alight by the fire of God."[39] In this sense Maurice is one of the most profoundly orthodox theologians of the nineteenth century, for his entire work is an attempt to express the ineffable mystery of God in fragile human language. "Systems, opinions, forms of society, may go," he exclaims, "but glory be to that which has been from age to age the refuge of the poor, the help of the needy, the Name of Truth and Love when they seemed banished from the world below. Glory be to the Father, and to the Son, and to the Holy Ghost. As it was in the beginning, is now, and ever shall be, world without end. Amen."[40]

NOTES

NOTES TO CHAPTER ONE

1. Stephen W. Sykes, *The Integrity of Anglicanism* (New York: Seabury Press, 1978), p. 35; ibid., p. 19.
2. Sykes, p. 34; ibid., p. 17.
3. H. P. Liddon, *The Life of Edward Bouverie Pusey*, 4 vols. (New York: Longmans, Green, 1893-97), 4:58.
4. R. G. Wilberforce, *Life of The Right Reverend Samuel Wilberforce, D.D.*, 3 vols. (London: n.p., 1880-82), 2:208ff.
5. Torben Christensen, *The Divine Order: A Study of F. D. Maurice's Theology* (Leiden: E. J. Brill, 1973), p. 22.
6. F. D. Maurice, *The Kingdom of Christ*, ed. Alec R. Vidler, 2 vols. (London: SCM Press, 1958), 1:18. This new edition is based on the second edition of 1842.
7. *Kingdom of Christ*, 1:58; cf. 1:42.
8. J. F. Porter and W. J. Wolf, eds., *Toward the Recovery of Unity* (New York: Seabury Press, 1964), p. 97.
9. *Recovery of Unity*, p. 104.
10. F. D. Maurice, *Lectures on the Ecclesiastical History of the First and Second Centuries* (London: Macmillan, 1854), p. 222.
11. *Kingdom of Christ*, 1:142.
12. *The Life of Frederick Denison Maurice*, ed. Frederick Maurice, 2 vols. (London: Macmillan, 1884), 2:137.
13. F. D. Maurice, *Moral and Metaphysical Philosophy, Part I*, 2d ed. rev. (London: J. J. Griffin, 1850), p. 150.
14. *Recovery of Unity*, p. 106.
15. *Life*, 1:518.
16. *Recovery of Unity*, p. 59.
17. *Life*, 2:137; ibid.
18. *Life*, 1:372; ibid., 2:137.
19. Ibid.

NOTES TO CHAPTER TWO

1. *Life*, 1:77.
2. *Women's Rights As Preached By Women*, by A Looker On (London: C. Kegan Paul, 1881), p. 56.
3. *Encyclopedia Britannica*, 11th ed., s.v. "Women."
4. Olive Brose, *Frederick Denison Maurice: Rebellious Conformist* (Athens, Ohio: Ohio University Press, 1971), p. 282.
5. *Kingdom of Christ* (1838), 3:288.
6. F. D. Maurice, "Female Education," *Metropolitan Quarterly Magazine*, II, No. 4, pp. 265-282; F. D. Maurice to Edmund Maurice, 4 January 1870, Maurice MSS (ADD 7793), Cambridge University Library, Cambridge University.
7. F. D. Maurice to (?-?) Jones, November 1815, Maurice MSS (ADD 7793).
8. *Life*, 1:14, 1:17.
9. Ibid., 1:43.
10. Ibid., 1:178.
11. Ibid., 1:264.
12. Annie Barton to F. D. Maurice, 20 July 1837, Maurice MSS (ADD 7793).
13. F. D. Maurice, *Eustace Conway: or The Brother and Sister*, 3 vols. (n.p., Richard Bentley, 1834), 2:916.
14. *Life*, 1:63-64.
15. F. D. Maurice, *Social Morality: twenty one lectures delivered in the University of Cambridge*, 2d ed. (London: Macmillan, 1872), pp. 62-63.
16. Ibid., pp. 54, 55.
17. Ibid., p. 79.
18. F. D. Maurice, "On Sisterhoods," *The Victoria Magazine*, I (August 1863): 289-301.

19. "Female Education"; F. D. Maurice, review of M. Ancey on Infant Education, *The Athenaeum*, 3 September 1828.
20. F. D. Maurice, "Female School of Art; Mrs. Jameson," *Macmillan's Magazine*, II, No. 9 (July 1860), p. 235.
21. Ibid., p. 234.
22. F. D. Maurice, *Queen's College, London: A Letter to the . . . Bishop of London* (London: J. W. Parker, 1850), p. 14.
23. *Life*, 1:87, 86.
24. F. D. Maurice to Sara Coleridge, 1843-1844, Relton Library, Bx 5037 — M4 — R, King's College, London.
25. F. D. Maurice, *Queen's College, London, its Objects and Methods* (London: F. J. Rivington, 1848), pp. 6, 8.
26. *Queen's College, London: A Letter*, p. 46.
27. F. D. Maurice, "Plan of a Female College for the Help of the Rich and the Poor," in *Lectures to Ladies on Practical Subjects* (London: Macmillan, 1855), p. 7.
28. Ibid., p. 12.
29. F. D. Maurice, "Personal Recollections of Women's Education," *Nineteenth Century*, August 1879, pp. 310-313.
30. *Social Morality*, p. 58.
31. F. D. Maurice, "Female Suffrage," *Spectator*, No. 2, 175 (March 1870), p. 298.
32. F. D. Maurice to Edmund Maurice, 4 January 1870, Maurice MSS (ADD 7793).
34. *Life*, 2:630. An examination of the relationship between Maurice and his second wife, Georgina Hare, would require more extensive space than is practicable in this chapter. They were married in what was supposed to be her last illness, but she was so pleased with her nuptials that she recovered after the ceremony and lived for nearly half a century afterward. She had been an invalid since childhood and, until his own last illness, Maurice watched over her with the most chivalrous de-

[89]

votion. "A rather cheeping body," Georgina Maurice is described by Maurice's close friend, John Malcolm Ludlow. Mrs. Maurice left her bed only rarely. Maurice served in a "feminine" capacity as her faithful nurse.

Maurice had also served as nurse to his sisters, Emma and Priscilla, who also rarely left their beds. With the exception of the seven years of his first marriage, Maurice was never freed from the care of chronically sick, doubtless neurotic, women. Perhaps this was a legitimate defensive device of the Victorian lady. Harriet Martineau, Florence Nightingale, not to mention Elizabeth Barrett Browning, all kept to their beds, sometimes for years at a time.

35. "Female Education," p. 266.
36. *Life*, 2:535.
37. Ibid., p. 643.
38. Ibid., p. 643.

NOTES TO CHAPTER THREE

1. *The Letters and Diaries of John Henry Newman*, ed. Charles Dessain and Edward E. Kelly, vol. 21 (London: Thomas Nelson and Sons, 1971), p. 504; F. W. Maitland, *The Life and Letters of Leslie Stephen* (London: Duckworth & Co., 1906), p. 240. For a representative sample of nineteenth-century views, see Alec Vidler, *F. D. Maurice and Company* (London: SCM Press, 1966), pp. 17-18.
2. See Charles E. Raven, *Christian Socialism*, 1848-1854 (London: Macmillan, 1920) and Torben Christensen's *The Divine Order* already cited, as well as his *Origins and History of Christian Socialism, 1848-1854*, trans. Bjerglund Andersen (Aarhus: Universitetsforlaget, 1962), Sykes, p. 19; Stephen

Pile, *The Incomplete Book of Failures* (New York: E. P. Dutton, 1979), p. 21.

3. *Life*, 2:292-293; Julia Wedgewood, *Nineteenth Century Teachers and Others* (London: Hodder & Stoughton, 1909), p. 29; Arthur Michael Ramsey, *F. D. Maurice and the Conflicts of Modern Theology* (Cambridge: Cambridge University Press, 1951), p. 40.

4. One of the few discussions on Maurice to recognize this devotional side to his work is A. M. Allchin, "F. D. Maurice as Theologian," *Theology* 76 (1973): 513-525. Allchin notes a similarity in this regard between Maurice and Richard Meaux Benson, founder of the Society of St. John the Evangelist.

5. *Tracts for the Times*, 5 vols. (London: F. & J. Rivington, 1840-42), 1:18, "Thoughts on the Benefits of the System of Fasting," p. 12; F. D. Maurice, *Tracts on Christian Socialism, No. 1: Dialogue between Somebody (A Person of Respectability) and Nobody (The Author)* (London: n.p., 1850), p. 10.

6. Among the attempts to create a cult of humanity were Saint-Simon's "New Christianity" and Auguste Comte's "Religion of Humanity."

7. *Kingdom of Christ*, 2:37.

8. F. D. Maurice, *Dialogues between a Clergyman and a Layman on Family Worship* (Cambridge and London: Macmillan, 1862), p. 212.

9. F. D. Maurice, *The Lord's Prayer, the Creed, and the Commandments* (London: Macmillan, 1870), p. viii; *Kingdom of Christ*, 1:254; F. D. Maurice, *The Prayer Book* (London: James Clarke & Co., 1966), p. 124.

10. *Prayer Book*, p. 85; *Family Worship*, p. 9.

11. F. D. Maurice, *Sermons Preached in Lincoln's Inn Chapel*, 6 vols. (London: Macmillan, 1891), 2:51; *Family Worship*, p. 216. Maurice regarded monastic communities as families, but

he warned that their survival in the Church of England would depend on their reverence for the biological families of which they were copies (see pp. 143-145).

12. *Kingdom of Christ*, 2:39; *Lincoln's Inn*, 2:13-14; *Prayer Book*, pp. 14-15; *Lincoln's Inn*, 4:132.
13. *Lord's Prayer*, p. 42.
14. *Prayer Book*, p. 200; *Kingdom of Christ*, 2:50.
15. Ibid., 1:265-266. The fact that the Book of Common Prayer teaches that we are made children of God in baptism did not trouble Maurice nearly as much as it did his critics. Human language could not do justice to God's saving grace, he believed. To Charles Kingsley he explained that rebirth was very much like natural birth: we are not changed into something new, but rather come under the influence of a love which already awaits us (*Life*, 1:214).
16. *Kingdom of Christ*, 2:142, 162; ibid., 2:48. Maurice's insistence on Christ's headship of the entire race is very different from the generally rigorist views of the Tractarians. But there are hints of the idea of general revelation in the early tracts, such as *Tracts for the Times*, 1:20, "Letters to a Friend, No. III," p. 1, and 2:47, "The Visible Church, Letter IV," p. 3.
17. *Life*, 1:188.
18. *Prayer Book*, p. 19; *Kingdom of Christ*, 2:43; ibid., 2:132-134; ibid., 1:283-285. See also *Tracts for the Times*, 2:67, "Scriptural Baptism," pp. 24, 27-28.
19. *Kingdom of Christ*, 1:270-271; *Lincoln's Inn*, 4:153.
20. *Lord's Prayer*, p. 19; *Kingdom of Christ*, 2:75.
21. F. D. Maurice, *The Eucharist: Five Sermons* (London: John E. Taylor, 1857), p. 91; *Kingdom of Christ*, 2:67; *Lincoln's Inn*, 4:114; *Prayer Book*, p. 134; *Lincoln's Inn*, 5:142.
22. Ibid., 4:16; *Kingdom of Christ*, 2:40-41.
23. *Lincoln's Inn*, 5:191; *Kingdom of Christ*, 2:42.

24. *Lincoln's Inn*, 2:59-77 *passim*; 4:155.
25. *Family Worship*, pp. 185-186.
26. *Kingdom of Christ*, 1:137, 2:39; *Lincoln's Inn*, 2:102.
27. *Kingdom of Christ*, 2:115-117; *Prayer Book*, p. 110; *Family Worship*, p. 167, and *Sermons Preached in Country Churches* (London: Macmillan, 1880), p. 5; *Kingdom of Christ*, 2:170-172, 180-181.
28. The most prominent "charismatic" sect in Victorian England was the Catholic Apostolic Church organized by disciples of Edward Irving; for his influence on Maurice, see Olive J. Brose, pp. 36-42; *Lincoln's Inn*, 4:16-18, 21-26. See also *Family Worship*, p. 186.
29. *Kingdom of Christ*, 2:42.
30. *Family Worship*, pp. 188-189.
31. Ibid., pp. 190-193, 122-123.
32. Ibid., pp. 194-196; *Kingdom of Christ*, 1:261-262.
33. *Country Churches*, p. 65; *Kingdom of Christ*, 2:77.
34. *Lincoln's Inn*, 3:209, and *Prayer Book*, pp. 108-109; *Lincoln's Inn*, 3:209-210; *Kingdom of Christ*, 1:277-278.
35. *Lincoln's Inn*, 4:130; *Eucharist*, p. 18; *Kingdom of Christ*, 2:59.
36. Ibid., 2:62-81 *passim*.
37. Ibid., 2:91; *Eucharist*, p. 41.
38. John Stuart Mill, *Autobiography* (New York: Columbia University Press, 1924), pp. 107-108.
39. Kenneth Leech, *True Prayer* (London: Sheldon Press, 1980), p. 11. The term "soul friend" has recently been popularized by his book of that name (Sheldon Press, 1977).
40. *Prayer Book*, p. 43.